The New Era of Real Estate

Gianluca Mattarocci • Xenia Scimone

The New Era of Real Estate

An Analysis of Business Models in the Proptech Industry

Gianluca Mattarocci
University of Rome Tor Vergata
Rome, Italy

Xenia Scimone
University of Rome Tor Vergata
Rome, Italy

ISBN 978-3-031-16730-0 ISBN 978-3-031-16731-7 (eBook)
https://doi.org/10.1007/978-3-031-16731-7

This Palgrave Macmillan imprint is published by the registered company Springer Nature Switzerland AG.
The registered company address is: Gewerbestrasse 11, 6330 Cham, Switzerland

Acknowledgment

The book has benefited greatly from comments provided by the anonymous reviewers who evaluated the book proposal. The quality of the final version would be significantly lower without the independent and high-quality review service provided by these academicians.

The book is the result of the authors' combined efforts and continuous exchange of ideas. Chapters 1, 2, 5, and 7 are ascribed to Xenia Scimone and the other chapters to Gianluca Mattarocci.

Special thanks to Alec Selwin, Tula Weiss, and all the staff at Palgrave Macmillan for their professional management of the review and the publication process.

CONTENTS

LIST OF FIGURES

LIST OF TABLES

CHAPTER 1

Introduction

Abstract Technology has changed the real estate market by offering new opportunities for satisfying customers' needs and new business models for competing in the market. New players are growing year by year, and the traditional companies were forced to adapt to the new competitive environment to survive in the real estate arena.

This chapter explains the book's structure and points out the originality of the approach proposed and the value added of the book concerning literature already available.

Keywords Proptech • Innovation • Real estate

New technologies are becoming part of almost every aspect of our everyday lives. Technological developments are transforming nearly every sector, and all sectors face the challenge of efficiently and successfully moving into a digital future. Any containment measures from the COVID-19 pandemic have accelerated the urgency. The real estate sector is no exception. For example, the search criteria of any house have changed, and the method of visiting properties for sale and rent has also changed. The agent discovered tools that already existed, such as virtual visits, which he did not use before because they did not represent a need for the user. Today user asks for quicker solutions, looking for speed as a critical aspect to satisfy their needs.

G. Mattarocci, X. Scimone, *The New Era of Real Estate*, https://doi.org/10.1007/978-3-031-16731-7_1

This book aims to analyze the issue of digitization applied to the real estate sector, understanding how it does impact the way companies adapt their business model and adopt new technologies to cope with more digitized sectors, which sets customers' expectations very high.

The word Proptech is composed of the terms "property" and "technology" and refers to all the technologies that are applied to the real estate and construction sector (KPMG, 2018; Shaw, 2018). Proptech is, on the one hand, the name under which the technological innovations that are developed and implemented in the property sector can be ascribed, but, on the other hand, also the industry itself, the business sector, or, more generally, the cultural movement within which this specific wave of innovation fits (Dearsley, 2018). It defines all start-ups that use technological innovations to provide solutions to real estate problems (Pyle et al., 2017).

Until a few years ago, it was little used; lately, it is widely used by industry experts and non-experts, thanks to its widespread use. In 2011, investments globally reached $186 million, and in 2017, they reached about $3 billion; in 2018, they skyrocketed to as much as $15 billion. In 2019, the global Proptech market reached a whopping $24.6 billion in investments. This is why defining Proptech as the simple application of technological tools to the real estate sector can be reductive: it must be considered a new philosophy or a new way of thinking about the real estate market.

There are two ways to explain the meaning of Proptech. The first explanation sees Proptech as a support tool: the use of methods, techniques, and tools that help in the real estate sector (Vandell & Green, 2010). This statement indicates that technology can facilitate work, improve work efficiency and effectiveness, and see innovation as an outcome characterized by the efficiency and effectiveness of the construction process (Kahn, 2018). The second meaning sees Proptech as a technique, method, or device that can change the property development process (KPMG, 2017; Lecamus, 2017). In this case, innovation is seen as a process characterized by a change in the development process of the product, services, management, and business models.

The advantages of using various technologies in the real estate sector are related to the growing benefits for consumers and developers working in the industry (Sim, 2017). There are opportunities and risks in the use of real estate technology (Maarbani, 2017): it can provide opportunities for developers to attract investors and to increase the participation of actors in the property development process, but on the other hand, there is a high risk of failure for developers using non-cutting edge technology if they do not increase their performance through innovation.

The technological transformation in the real estate sector includes a set of technologies applied to it, such example, innovative homes services such as Alexa or similar, real estate platforms for sale and rent, data analysis tools, Artificial Intelligence, Blockchain, and a list could still be very long (Siniak et al., 2020). Proptech encompasses all types of businesses related to technological improvements in the real estate sector. Start-ups and companies can be classified as protected even if the activities are unrelated, sometimes causing misunderstandings in using the term. All these innovations can improve productivity and competitiveness, increase the energy efficiency of the resources used, and consequently protect the environment, providing opportunities for economic growth for both developed and developing countries (UNIDO, 2017). So, when we talk about Proptech, we are not limited to the real estate market only. Still, we consider other areas such as smart cities, intelligent buildings, the sharing economy applied to real estate, the residential construction industry, Contech, the Blockchain, co-working and co-living, and crowdfunding referring to new installations and real estate investments.

These relatively recent innovations can improve productivity and competitiveness, increase energy and resource efficiency and effectiveness, protect the environment, and provide opportunities for developed and developing countries to achieve economic growth and sustainable development.

Three aspects are important to consider the implications that Proptech has had in the field of governance. First, Proptech increases the enormous amount of information recorded on land, homes, and properties. Second, data digitization has specific effects ranging from emerging digital data as an asset with value in and of itself to data susceptible to algorithmic analysis. Third, Proptech brings new players, products, and services to the housing and real estate sectors, which translates into a consequent increase in competition and, therefore, efficiency in the industry (Porter et al., 2019).

Digitization in the sector leads to increased transactions related to the sale and rental of properties. The Blockchain applied to the real estate sector adds liquidity to the market and simplifies a property's purchase or sale process.

Digitalization with legal value through Blockchain and automation through smart contracts, the acts and transitions then indicate to the sector real estate a promising prospect, as it could materialize a significant reduction in both execution times and management costs and conservation, also increasing the guarantees of authenticity of the documents and their not "falsifiability." In fact, an operation that generally takes months to be completed was completed within a few hours. Compared to current standards, Blockchain technology seems to ensure more incredible speed, higher levels of trust and security, and complete transparency for all participants, including any person who issues a loan to support the operation.

Artificial intelligence tools make it possible to better geolocalize an asset by assigning a correct value concerning its position. Even the most immediate access to information, integrated with data from all potential sources and the support of indicators on the current state of the property, will benefit professionals in the sector and those who have to make economic decisions—managerial. The immediate financial impact of the intelligent management of services and related data will allow real estate professionals to increase and improve their real estate portfolio management activities. Let's not forget how today, 70% of the costs of a property are related to its management.

Given all these advantages, it is easy to understand how the real estate sector, thanks to technological innovation, currently represents an important and exciting business for investors. In particular, thanks to the use of the Blockchain in the context of transactions for the circulation of property, thanks to tour services through virtual reality, thanks to the use of specific 3D technology for the real estate sector, Proptech is a sector destined to grow, also testified by the fact that many venture capital funds are being created fully dedicated to this new business model.

But, there are difficulties in the growth of the sector, such as:

- lack of technological culture,
- the low propensity for real estate,
- lack of a Proptech ecosystem.

The coronavirus pandemic has only partially hurt the business: 25% of Proptech companies have found new development opportunities, thanks to COVID-19.

The real estate sector was significantly affected by the pandemic emergency, starting from the hotel sector, commercial, and offices, both in the phase of greatest stasis and the subsequent restart. During the pandemic crisis, companies in the real estate sector were among those that most all have declared that they had experienced an acceleration of investment. In fact, on average, it was observed that real estate companies invested in the adoption and implementation of new digital tools more than 10% of their budget. Above all, real estate companies between 5 and 10 years of activity have pushed the digitization accelerator.

In any case, the risks should certainly not be underestimated. The growth of the technological level implies the need to raise the continuity requirements operational and countering cyber threats. A proliferation of solutions Distributed Ledger can also increase market fragmentation, damaging the comparability of offers and the protection of users. The more general risk is complexity, given that the market real estate manages not only economic and financial needs but also families' material, social and emotional needs. Neither does it follow that the technology used for this part of the market will have to be simple and such to avoid the company's fringes that may remain on the edges of the new digital world.

In the following book, we want to provide a representation of Proptech. Indeed, we do not have the presumption of offering a complete and exhaustive picture as, as previously mentioned, the phenomenon of Proptech is vast. It affects many aspects of people's lives, regulators, fintech, etc. However, being still little treated by academics to date, we wanted to write a book about it, providing the critical points of the new real estate finance.

The book consists of six chapters in total, including an introduction.

The second chapter aims to analyze the phenomenon of Proptech, focusing on its evolution over the years, the advantages and disadvantages of applying technological innovation to the real estate sector on the new business models of companies employed in the real estate sector. Finally, through market analysis, we tried to identify the state of Proptech at the beginning of 2021 by identifying 633 companies active in the industry.

The third chapter, on the other hand, aims to analyze the Proptech services offered for the management of properties with a focus on data and experiences related to European realities. Or rather, the individual risks that characterize a real estate investment and the possible solutions offered by Proptech will be examined in detail.

The fourth chapter will consider the negotiation stage and all the solutions offered by the new technology to speed up the process and reduce the transaction risk related to information asymmetry.

In the fifth chapter, we analyze how crowdfunding and P2P lending work in general terms, then go down precisely on the two alternatives that can be used for financing in real estate: debt crowdfunding and equity crowdfunding.

In the end, we provide the main conclusions concerning the main characteristics of Proptech analyzed in the previous chapters.

REFERENCES

Dearsley, J. (2018) *What is PropTech?* Retrieved November 7, from http://www. jamesdearsley.co.uk/what-is-proptech/

Kahn, K. B. (2018). Understanding innovation. *Business Horizons, 61,* 453–460.

KPMG Global PropTech Survey. (2017). *Bridging the gap: how the real estate sector can engage with PropTech to bring the built and digital environments together.* KPMG International.

KPMG. (2018). *KPMG Global Proptech Survey.* KPMG.

Lecamus, V. (2017). PropTech: What is it and how to address the new wave of real estate startups?

Maarbani, S. (2017). *Real estate technology: Threat or opportunity.* White Paper: The future of RealTech.

Porter, L., Fields, D., Landau-Ward, A., Rogers, D., Sadowski, J., Maalsen, S., Kitchin, R., Dawkins, O., Young, G., & Bates, L. K. (2019). PropTech and housing – the view from Melbourne/digital housing and renters. *Planning Theory & Practice.* https://doi.org/10.1080/14649357.2019.1651997

Pyle, A., Grunewald, D., & Wright, N. (2017). *Bridging the gap. How the real estate sector can engage with PropTech to bring the built and digital environments together* (pp. 1–24).

Shaw, J. (2018). Platform real estate: Theory and practice of new urban real estate markets. *Urban Geography.* https://doi.org/10.1080/02723638.2018. 1524653

Sim, D. (2017). *Property technology: Disruptor or enabler?* CBRE Research.

Siniak, N., Kauko, T., Shavrov, S., & Marina, M. (2020). *The impact of proptech on real estate industry growth.* IOP Conference Series: Materials Science and Engineering, Vol. 869, Management in Construction.

UNIDO. (2017). *Opportunities and challenges of the new industrial revolution for developing countries and economies in transition.* Panel discussion online. https://www.unido.org/sites/default/files/2017-01/Unido_industry-4_NEW_0.pdf

Vandell, K. D., & Green, R. K. (2010). *The impact of technology on commercial real estate.* Urban Land Economics Research.

CHAPTER 2

The Evolution of Proptech

Abstract Proptech history started in the 80s when technology and the World Wide Web entered the real estate market for the first time. During the last decades, new instruments and solutions were developed, and nowadays, the proptech segments and business models are frequently changing to adapt to the latest market scenario.

This chapter presents the evolution of the market over time and focuses the attention on Proptech 3.0 and the role of Blockchain in innovating the business model. By focusing on the EU27 market, the chapter also proposes an analysis of the difference in the market size and growth perspectives in different countries.

Keywords Proptech • Contech • Fintech • Blockchain • Business model

2.1 Introduction

Companies are studying and investing billions of dollars in changing how real estate is traded, used, and managed on the market. During the last decade, we are experiencing a significant change in the modus operandi of the real estate sector; a sector historically has been subject to only a few or at least prolonged changes even if it represents a significant economic activity for each country. Real estate's role in the global economy is

G. Mattarocci, X. Scimone, *The New Era of Real Estate*,
https://doi.org/10.1007/978-3-031-16731-7_2

undeniable, and often changes/shacks in this sector are used as a leading indicator to assess the growth of a country's economy. At the European level, the market has reached its peak: almost one-fifth of GDP is based on the real estate sector, and Italy is among the top five countries for the role of companies active in the industry (19% of GDP), and about 80% of the wealth of Italians is made up of real estate.

In recent decades, industry-related improvements are moving toward increasing the use of technology to improve efficiency, reduce production and trading costs, and improve customer satisfaction.

Digitization in real estate is developing very slowly compared to other sectors due to the low elasticity that characterizes this market: a change in the demand of users (e.g., on the characteristics of the property) takes a long time to be absorbed and implemented by the industry and therefore reflected on the change in supply.

The Proptech phenomenon has emerged as the culmination of years of development, finance, and innovation focused on transparency, participation, and understanding of the real estate industry (KPMG, 2018).

This multidisciplinary approach has evolved into a profitable industry (Forbes, 2018; Shaw, 2018), and literature has identified three periods of the evolution based on the customers' target needs (Baum, 2017):

1. Consumer target;
2. Small businesses and new technology;
3. New business models (Table 2.1).

The following chapter aims to analyze the evolution of proptech over the years, focusing on activities, technology applications, business models, and new trends related to using Blockchain and cryptocurrencies.

2.2   PROPTECH 1.0 (1982–2000)

In the beginning, technology was applied to real estate identified through the era of Proptech 1.0, which began around the mid-1980s in the United States and the United Kingdom (Baum, 2017). The critical factors of the change were the introduction of personal computers and floppy disks in the late 1970s and early 1980s, which allowed for more precise and complex processing of data on computer spreadsheets, significantly changing the approach to analysis and research. These innovations, together with

Table 2.1 Proptech's evolution

	Baum
Proptech 1.0	1980–2000 Informatization data Computer Internet Es: Autodesk
Proptech 2.0	2000–until today Retail real estate online E-commerce and online platforms Social networks Es: Zoopla, Zillow
Proptech 3.0	2017 and then Disintermediation Blockchain Bitcoin and smart contract Es: Securrency, Ethereum

Source: Authors' elaboration

the growth of the Real Estate Investment Trust (REIT) in terms of investors, capital, and consulting services, have stimulated the growth of Information and Communications Technology (ICT) in real estate producing new opportunities for growth and development in the sector.

Despite technology innovations, the storage and transfer of a large amount of data was always a problem, as was its accessibility to the population. Even in the real estate sector, there was an increasing need to process a large amount of data rapidly, a problem highlighted in particular between the mid-1980s and the end of the 1980s due to the economic boom.

The growth of indirect real estate investment and the rapid globalization of the real estate sector in terms of investors, capital sources, and consulting services have led to a greater demand for more computers capable of carrying out rapid and consistent analysis.

Alongside these developments, e-commerce had become increasingly popular in the rest of the world, followed by the use of email in the 1990s, which facilitated the transfer of files via email and the storage of a large amount of data analysis (Coffman & Odlyzko, 2001). This technological expansion led to the creation of companies such as Craigslist in the United States and Exchange and Mart in the United Kingdom that sold and rented properties to a growing online audience paving the way for e-commerce in the real estate and financial sector.

After the introduction of the personal computer and later with the spread of tools such as Lotus and Excel, real estate institutions began to adopt technology to guide more quantitative approaches to investment and portfolio management. Software companies have emerged to meet the demand for better tools to support essential industry functions such as accounting and market analysis. Unlike the business software solutions we see today, the products introduced during this period were closed-form business services that did not communicate or integrate and, in many cases, required expensive customization by the end user.

In both the United States and the United Kingdom, real estate research companies such as Investment Property Databank (IPD) (1985) and Prudential (1987) have not only acted in the real estate investment sector, but the engineering and construction industries have also benefited from these advances (Ojo et al., 2018). Autodesk, Costar, Argus, Loopnet, and Yardi were software developed to provide architecture support and construction management. Technology-based companies have established themselves by providing seemingly complete business services, often requiring strong customer service customization and high-cost support. However, they were not open or collaborative companies (Fig. 2.1).

In the early years of the new millennium, the collapse of telecommunications triggered by investors, aware that the transmission and processing capacity had exceeded mainly the demand for information because too expensive, has led many companies in the sector to bankruptcy.

Market cap: $28,8B	Market cap: $13,0B (NASDAQ:CSGP)	Market cap: Acquired by Altus (TSE: AIF $969M)	Valuation: Acquired by CoStar for $624,4m	Market cap: n/a
AUTODESK	**CoStar Group**	**ARGUS** SOFTWARE *an Altus Group company*	**LoopNet**	**YARDI**
Founded: 1982 (NASDAQ: ADSK) Product: Software for the architecture, engineering and construction	Founded: 1987 Product: Provider of CRE data, analytics, marketing services	Founded: 1985 Product: Software for CRE underwriting	Founded: 1995 Product: CRE database	Founded: 1984 Product: Software for CRE accounting & back-office

Fig. 2.1 First software was developed to support the real estate sector. Source: Authors' elaboration on 2021 annual report data

Table 2.2   Data exchange in the United States at the end of 2000

Network	Traffic (TB/month)
United States voice	53,000
Internet	20,000–35,000
Other public data networks	3000
Private line	6000–11,000

Source: Coffman and Odlyzko (2001)

The period between 1980 and 2000 was called Proptech 1.0. It suffered an oversupply of real estate computer technology because it was expensive and not collaborative, lacking adequate traffic demand (Baum, 2017) (Table 2.2).

2.3   PROPTECH 2.0 (2001–2016)

After the dot-com boom, the Internet era inaugurated a new period of consumer confidence in online transactions. At the beginning of Proptech 1.0, it was difficult to find real estate information online and almost impossible to buy or rent a house without first having a physical encounter between the parties.

In the early 2000s, large online aggregators emerged in the social media and e-commerce sectors, making consumers more comfortable making online transactions in the real estate sector. Online portals such as Zillow and Trulia have aimed to take advantage of the opportunity provided by residential properties, given the relative size and availability of data. These teams have begun to "disintegrate" existing information providers by exploiting new technological breakthroughs such as the cloud and mobile devices increasingly popular. With decreasing costs, Wi-Fi and 4G have become reference platforms in the industry (Fig. 2.2).

This new approach used by the platforms, linked to the increased demand for rental housing and the need to make sales and purchases of real estate more efficient, led to the evolution of Proptech 1.0, defined as Proptech 2.0, which started in the new millennium (ING, 2018).

Thanks to significant advances in data processing, storage, and management, the years between 2008 and 2018 have led some companies in proptech to rapidly develop and acquire more and more market share. Consumers' preference for the use of a property over the ownership of the

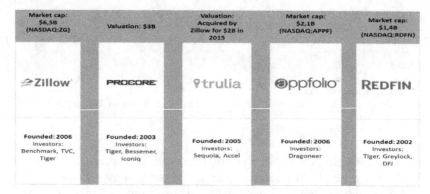

Fig. 2.2 Software developed to support real estate in the years 2000. Source: Authors' elaboration on 2021 data annual report data

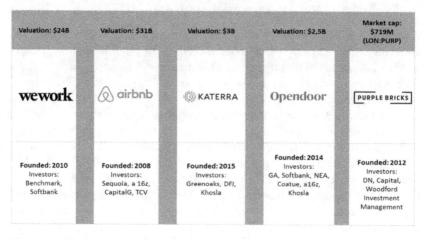

Fig. 2.3 The first companies born in Proptech 2.0. Source: Authors' elaboration on 2021 annual report data

same has pushed companies such as WeWork and Airbnb to make a comprehensive way in the industry. These companies have exploited the sharing economy to create more fungible physical spaces, including homes, offices, and retail stores. Companies in the Proptech 2.0 era sought to improve the user experience toward renting, buying, selling, and building real estate (Fig. 2.3).

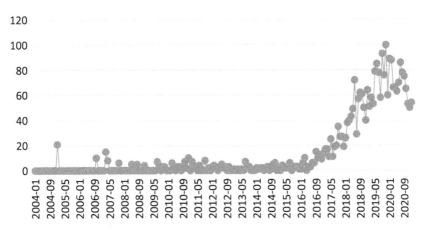

Fig. 2.4 Interest vs. Proptech 2.0 worldwide between 2004 and 2021. Notes: The number represents the interest toward the term "Proptech" on the searches Google, calculated relative to the point of interest highest in the time. The value 100 represents the peak of popularity for the term over time. Value 50 indicates average popularity over the peak. Source: Google Trends—https://trends.google. com/trends/explore?date=all&q=proptech

Customers gradually became more dissatisfied with the property purchasing experience as they demanded that these properties incorporate "intelligent" technology. There is a new demand from consumers, and data show that the word "proptech" has grown in interest among Internet users (Fig. 2.4).

2.3.1 Proptech Segments

The complexity of understanding and classifying Proptech enterprises stems from the significant number of emerging companies related to the industry and the differences between them that are not well defined or currently consolidated.

Proptech is part of a larger digital ecosystem that interconnects with fintech and could be divided into three sectors according to vertical criteria: Smart real estate, Shared economy, and Real estate Fintech (Fig. 2.5).

Intelligent real estate finance (Smart real estate) includes digital platforms that facilitate the operation and management of a property, thus making it a "smart building." An intelligent building usually refers to a

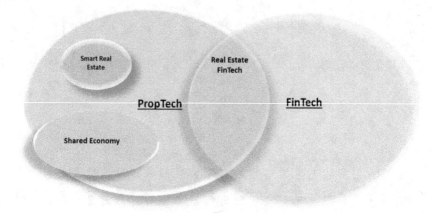

Fig. 2.5 Proptech sectors classification. Source: Authors' elaboration

resource that works efficiently through automated technology. A "space" for residents and users that, integrated with new technologies, can increase efficiency, for example, in regulating energy heating in space and the sustainable use of water, air, and gas.

From the shared economy (shared economy) perspective, technology-based real estate platforms facilitate using real estate assets. It usually refers to co-working and co-living and is defined as the sharing or exchange through peer-to-peer platforms of real estate or related services. The most notable examples of shared economy platforms are Airbnb and We-Work. Airbnb is an American platform that deals with booking and renting a private residential property.

Real Estate Fintech focuses on digital platforms that facilitate real estate asset trading and includes property search sites, crowdfunding platforms, P2P mortgage comparison technology platforms, search engines for leases, and property management.

Among the horizontal segments of Proptech, the following activities are distinguished:

- provision/making available of information;
- facilitation of transactions;
- control and management of the property.

Table 2.3   The intersections between horizontal and vertical criteria in Proptech

	Real estate Fintech	*Shared economy*	*Smart real estate*
Information	Yes	Yes	Yes
Transactions/market	Yes	Yes	
Control and management			Yes

Source: Authors' elaboration

Vertical and horizontal criteria intersect in a way that is not perfectly two-way, according to the interpretation proposed by Baum (Table 2.3):

- Real Estate Fintech, Shared Economy, and Smart Real Estate all intersect with the theme of information;
- the facilitation of transactions pertains to Fintech Real Estate and the Shared Economy, but not to Smart Real Estate;
- control and management mainly refer to Smart Real Estate.

It is also important to underline that this classification excludes technological platforms that support the design or construction of buildings or infrastructures, considering this type of activity as "Contech" even if they are technological platforms that support the real estate sector (in the construction/design phases). Baum's classification does not consider them as Proptechs (ING, 2018).

Shaw (2018) suggests a different approach to defining Proptech by arguing that traditional classification into market segments seemed confusing and problematic. Therefore, consider Proptech as a sum of digital platforms interconnecting various real estate stakeholders. It provides a different platform view: platforms bring "things" together in temporary aggregations, adding value to both things and the platform itself. Rather than classifying digital real estate platforms, it identifies stakeholders into four clusters by illustrating their interrelation (Fig. 2.6).

Each circle in Fig. 2.6 is assigned a different market stakeholder, while the circle's size indicates the respective stakeholder's role in the real estate sector. The links between the processes represent digital platforms, and the width of each link shows the amount of digital media available.

In cluster 1, the types of platforms included typically offer a range of information, products, and data analytics to help investment fund managers, asset fund managers, and those with capital make buy/sell best decisions that include:

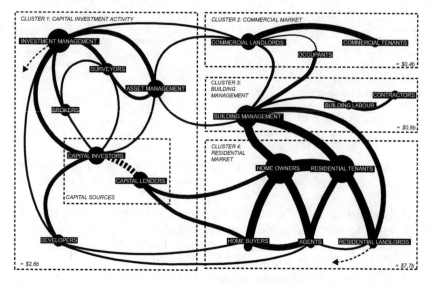

Fig. 2.6 A new classification of Proptech. Source: Shaw (2018)

- a series of data science and financial management products that have been aggregated and linked in online dashboards;
- data services such as API and "data warehouse";
- crowd-investing platforms that link sources of capital to real estate ownership.

These platforms, therefore, connect market stakeholders with information that allows them to make decisions related to capital investments in the real estate sector and profit-seeking, especially for significant funds with a high net worth. They are generally aimed at huge investors (investment funds, REITs, etc.) even if the aggregation of data deriving from various sources also allows small investors and agents to monitor and research the best market opportunities, albeit of smaller properties.

Cluster 2 represents the commercial real estate market: platforms where investors or funds are the owners of commercial properties who need to connect to their tenants, users, and building managers.

Cluster 3 is the area of building management and platforms operating between the residential and commercial markets.

Cluster 4 represents the residential market and comprises a relatively large number of platforms operating there and dealing with: home sales, vacation rental, tenant verification and screening services, and real estate agents.

What stands out is that real estate agents are not among the dominant stakeholders in a real estate transaction. Furthermore, the connection between homeowners and residential tenants is direct and bypasses agents.

Shaw (2018) and Baum (2017) agree that Proptech, in one way or another, represents various digital platforms that impact the real estate sector, including the real estate brokerage sector.

Finally, some authors provide a different segmentation of Proptech, including the following categories that can be impacted (ING, 2018; Venture Scanner, 2016):

- management system;
- product research;
- documentation;
- property insurance;
- shared economy;
- Smart Real Estate;
- investment management and property financing;
- services related to the property.

These categories are organized according to their functions in the real estate sector and offer specialized services related to data management, transactions, services, and controls.

Technologies related to data help in their storage, retrieval, management, and display.

Transaction-related real estate technology facilitates the process of exchanging products and services in the industry.

The Proptech connected to the services and control functions represents the use of technology in the management, control, and acquisition of services in the real estate sector to improve the performance of the products (very useful, in particular, in the management process in the post-construction phase).

Similarly, in Baum (2017) and Shaw (2018), RICS (2017) considers digital platforms as a predominant trend in the real estate sector that has a significant impact on the traditional approach to real estate brokerage. These digital platforms fall under Proptech 2.0 and Proptech 3.0, respectively. Furthermore, with technological progress, it is possible to identify three different groups of platforms that have a growing direct impact on disintermediation in real estate transactions.

1. The largest group of platforms on the market is websites that advertise properties. They do not lead to disintermediation but represent a valuable tool for the first meeting between supply and demand (Conway, 2019; Alfaraj, 2019).
2. Another group, also called "iBuyers," which has recently emerged in the United States, is made up of web platforms that buy the property directly from the seller, renovate it, and advertise it to potential buyers (Moore, 2018).
3. The third group comprises the recently appeared real estate technology companies aiming to completely disintermediate conventional brokers (Choi et al., 2019). They offer services similar to traditional real estate agents and act as an online intermediary between sellers and buyers. Low costs and high-quality service are at the heart of their business model (Ullah et al., 2018; Bughin & Van Zeebroeck, 2017; Read, 2019). A distinctive feature of this group is the close specialization that does not allow.

Based on the above evidence, it was noted that Proptech is prominent in developed economies. There is less evidence of Proptech developing in less profitable markets. Moore (2018) suggests that this could result from a poorly regulated market, lack of data transparency, and the non-existence of real estate institutions.

Fuster et al. (2019) suggest that because many buyers are not comfortable interacting only with digital real estate companies, the technology will not completely replace human interaction at the home buying stage and is likely to coexist and integrate "face-to-face" transactions. However, to coexist, real estate brokerage stakeholders must adapt quickly and embrace new technologies by changing their business strategy (Chircu & Kauffman, 2000). Failing to adapt rapidly to new market conditions, traditional intermediaries are likely to experience a significant impact on their revenues and profits, leading to the obsolescence of conventional real estate brokerage in the future (Devaney et al., 2017; Law et al., 2015).

2.3.2   Business Model in the Proptech Industry

Technology has allowed protecting operators from changing the business model of traditional players to take advantage of the benefits associated with using online channels and make their service different and more innovative.

The first solution adopted to maximize the number of potential customers is not to offer an all-inclusive commission for all the services offered but to segment customers by providing them the possibility to choose the level of service required (more or less complete) and to have a different price depending on the commitment needed for the different phases of the real estate investment. In this case, less sophisticated customers will be interested in having a complete service. They will agree to pay high fees, while the more advanced customers will make a cost comparison concerning competitors active on the market by selecting only the services that are offered at conditions in line or better than the market (Gee, 2010).

The success and customer satisfaction of proptech companies depend on the customer's confidence in using Internet channels and the ability to provide high-added value services that justify the cost (Littlefield et al., 2000). Firms that offer trading, management, and financing services have consequently invested in developing technologies and platforms that make it possible to use information remotely (from mobile phones or other devices) and in real-time.

Firms operating on real estate transactions have significantly reduced their profit margins because the cost and time required to collect valuable information to carry out a contract have shrunk dramatically (Zumpano et al., 2003). The relevance of the proptech segment is more significant for the lower-value properties segment, in which the customer is mainly interested in minimizing service costs and is willing to accept low-value-added services based on the use of technological tools finding online spaces through which to rent or buy a property was unimaginably or, in any case, very difficult before Proptech 1.0. The information on a property was centered on real estate agents: even a tiny agent could "survive" on the market for a year or more by closing only a few transactions. Nowadays, the properties are searchable on the Internet through individual brokers' sites and on sites that aggregate the information and data of multiple brokers. For example, the Proptech 1.0 were born: CoStar and LoopNet (owned by CoStar), startups RealMassive, TheSquareFoot, Hubble, and Property Works, SPD, Xceligent, REALLY, and Real Capital

Markets. Not all of these will remain on the market even in the era of Proptech 3.0.

In the pre-digital era, companies could offer a service based on a local market largely detached from other markets due to geographical remoteness (Forman et al., 2018). This changes with the digital platform business model as users can switch between digital platforms without much effort.

The use of online channels for property management in Proptech 2.0 determines the need for the protected company to invest in the technology necessary for data protection and the management of any legal disputes with suppliers or customers operating in other jurisdictions. The solutions adopted to manage any legal problems are to concentrate negotiations in a few countries and, in particular cases, to apply restrictions on access to the service for companies located in countries where there is a high degree of uncertainty in the legislation to protect contracts (Aalberts & Haila, 2018).

Furthermore, since traditional brokers want to attract the broadest possible user base, they will offer the critical services for free. They will have to adapt their business model to digital platforms to be competitive in the market. However, providing the service through digital media, despite the marginal costs close to zero, is expensive: a critical server infrastructure is required to manage the web-trac, data centers, archive relevant data, a team of IT engineers, web designers, and customer service specialists to keep the website running smoothly and provide the best user experience. Therefore, we currently see business dynamics centered on information and data technology. These business models collect, aggregate, and process information digitally. For companies, the report provides a valuable starting point for decisions to make (particularly regarding new products or services to offer to customers) or to implement automated valuation models (AVMs) (Brynjolfsson & Mitchell, 2017). A platform like Zoopla could then decide to sell the data to other companies or use it to attract an even larger user base. If the venue has a vibrant database, the AVM of the platform will likely perform better than other valuation models on the market as it has been developed on a large set of information. It is in such a situation that data becomes the actual value of the company:

Finally, operators' success in the online real estate financing market is linked to their reputation as it is necessary to attract new potential investors and select customers of good standing (Gibilaro, 2016). The intermediaries operating in this sector are consequently characterized by more significant investment in the promotion necessary for fundraising campaigns, good transparency on the operations carried out in the past and the relative performances, and the investment acquisition of resources in guarantee instruments which, in the event of bankruptcy of some funded initiatives, they reimburse investors pro-rata and consequently reduce the perceived risk of investing in proptech.

2.4   PROPTECH 3.0

Proptech 3.0 is based on the recent development of Blockchain technology. It is a beautiful approach, especially for a private market, such as real estate (Baum, 2017), characterized by transactions requiring time, physical proximity, and interpersonal relationships. The Blockchain, therefore, represents a turning point in commerce as it has the potential to purchase a home "online" through "smart contracts." This would eliminate paper contracts and simplify the process saving thousands of dollars.

Furthermore, technology can drastically change the way buildings are used. In many parts of Asia, homes are no longer considered mere residences to house people. Intelligent technology and the Internet of Things help home users in all their activities, from monitoring their residents/users to managing their appliances.

The Blockchain applied to the real estate sector adds liquidity to this market, simplifying a property's purchase or sale process. With the Blockchain, it is possible that several people, often very distant from each other, purchase a share of the same property, investing in it or sharing ownership even remotely, bypassing intermediaries.

Proptech 3.0 aims to revolutionize the real estate market by bringing a high disruption to the sector. The technologies associated with Proptech 3.0 are (Ullah et al., 2018; Baum, 2017; Shaw, 2018):

– Blockchain: allows the secure and transparent registration of real estate securities and provides faster turnaround times in transactions, as well as improving the liquidity and indivisibility of assets (Wessels, 2016);
– Big Data: contributes to the reduction of the risks associated with the purchase of property and allows to profile the consumer, better analyzing his habits and tastes, supporting companies in making decisions and adopting winning strategies that can better satisfy the consumer expectations (Mathew et al., 2015);

- Artificial Intelligence (AI)—can quickly manage multiple properties and improve customer interaction. Furthermore, artificial intelligence can rapidly advance the census of vast territories. The geolocation of an asset allows you to assign a value to the property concerning its position, quickly identifying criteria to estimate the value of its future sale (Ullah et al., 2018);
- Internet of Things (IoT): keeps users more immersed and connected to the built environment (Li et al., 2009);
- Cloud Computing and Software as a Service (SaaS): reduce IT costs in organizations (Dawson, 2016);
- Virtual Reality Software and Hardware: they increase and offer the possibility of viewing the properties by not physically visiting them;
- Drones: create more significant attraction for customers by providing overhead shots of real estate projects. They can map the territory from a different perspective and make the consumer visit a property in virtual mode even before construction has begun (Kuzma et al., 2017).

While some technologies are developed to enhance the business of real estate brokers, others bring disruptive innovations intended to disintermediate traditional brokers (Yasav, 2015).

A vision of the development of Proptech was proposed by RICS (2017), where it is observed how the various real estate stakeholders digitize their way of doing business over time (Fig. 2.7).

RICS (2017) stresses that Proptech and digitization are not exclusively about purchasing software or IT equipment but integrating them into companies' business processes, changing how they plan, build, maintain, and use social media and economic infrastructure.

In other words, we are witnessing the birth and development of the Proptech 3.0 era. Emerging technologies like 3D printing and cryptocurrencies are poised to make further forays into real estate.

Not too far in the future, entire buildings could be 3D printed. Singapore's Nanyang Technological University is studying how to use giant 3D printers to "print" whole levels of a skyscraper. China's WinSun already claims to have printed a five-story building with decorative elements inside.

In the future, companies will automate processes, and new tools will emerge to offer recommendations to support investment decisions. The

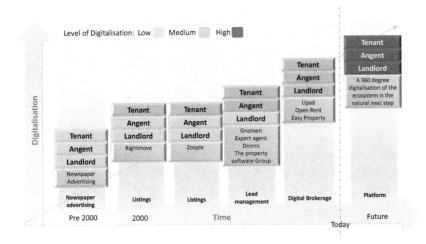

Fig. 2.7 The development of Proptech according to RICS. Source: Authors' elaboration

evolution of asset management and analysis will encourage the real estate sector to provide more and more online services. Interest in Proptech is already significantly increasing (Fig. 2.8).

Indeed, real estate has remained one of the least flexible sectors, which has rejected digitalization and technological innovation in many respects, particularly regarding the transfer of ownership and enjoyment rights over the asset.

What is clear is that things will change and also rapidly. Obviously, as in all sectors, applying technology to real estate opens up the debate on legal issues.

In the use of virtual reality applied to real estate and 3D printing, one of the questions that emerged is that related to the ownership of the software code and databases (considering that much of the code used is open source), to the sharing of information collected through such software and their secure deletion. The main issue concerns the potential increase in cyber attacks and, therefore, the risk of data loss and the loss of confidentiality.

The guarantee of people's privacy and the high standards of IT security will undoubtedly be challenges that the real estate sector will have to face shortly.

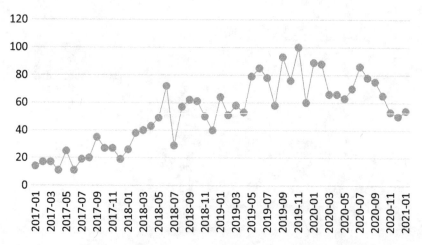

Fig. 2.8 Interest vs. Proptech 3.0—around the world. Note: The number represents the interest in the term "Proptech" on Google searches, calculated relative to the highest point of interest over time. The value 100 represents the peak of popularity for the term period. A value of 50 indicates medium popularity compared to the maximum peak. Source: Google Trends—https://trends.google.com/trends/explore?date=all&q=proptech

2.4.1   Blockchain Technology

The Blockchain can be defined as a decentralized database (a sort of transaction register where data is not stored on a single computer but on multiple machines connected via the Internet), structured in blocks of data, each containing a certain amount of information and distributed through a "chain" (i.e., a ledger) over a network. Hence, it is a digital way to store any type of data across a network (Morabito, 2017; Walport, 2016).

In particular, the Blockchain is a distributed network, which means that the data contained in the ledger is constantly shared and synchronized among its participants, even if they are spread across multiple sites, institutions, or geographical areas. Each participant in the network can access the shared recordings. It is a simple and ingenious system simultaneously to pass information from A to B entirely automatically and safely.

The peculiarity of the Blockchain is that it does not have a central authority: by its very definition, it is a decentralized, democratized, and transparent system that bases its functioning on the relationship of trust established between the users of the network. Since the ledger is shared and immutable, all information it contains is accessible to anyone.

Another of the main features of this technology is its security, as the validation and storage of data are not performed by a single central entity (as it can be for traditional financial intermediaries) but by numerous "nodes" that are part of the network. Nodes are computers that are connected to the network, participate in the transaction verification process, transmit the new blocks to the Blockchain, and keep an updated copy of the entire register. All nodes perform these operations simultaneously, so the more their number grows, the more secure the system is, as a cyber attack on a single node would not affect the chain.

Finally, another distinctive feature of the Blockchain is the complete transparency of its transactions and information. For this reason, the Blockchain's paradigm shift mainly concerns the concept of trust: it allows transactions to be carried out in the open, favoring trust between two parties operating a transaction (Fig. 2.9).

Uses and Advantages of the Blockchain
As mentioned, the areas of application and benefits of the Blockchain are many and potentially infinite, and the main application areas are:

1. Money transfers are carried out with the help of cryptocurrencies—these are incredibly safe and cost-free transactions;
2. Smart contracts: they are impartial and neutral toward all the parties involved as they are not influenced by human emotions and have no personal interest as they work through algorithms;

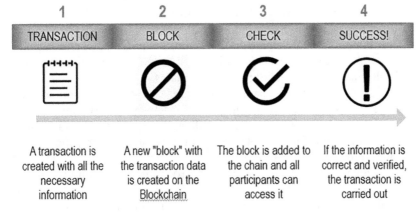

Fig. 2.9   The Blockchain process. Source: Authors' elaboration

3. Avoid exposure to hackers and violation of privacy: a Blockchain is an essential tool for verifying information. What is added to the Blockchain remains there permanently and immutably, so the identities cannot be stolen or altered since there is only one identity for each person/object in the Blockchain ledger;
4. It allows knowing the exact origin of all the parts that make up a product, and this benefits producers who understand the basis of their raw materials and final consumers.

Two aspects of Blockchain technology have been very popular with start-up founders and private equity firms worldwide. First, Blockchain could make the infrastructure of the financial services industry much less expensive. Second, the list of potential uses is almost unlimited. Blockchain systems could be much cheaper than existing platforms because they remove an entire layer of overhead dedicated to confirming authenticity. Everyone does the confirmation of the transaction on the network at the same time. This "consensus" process reduces the need to work alongside existing intermediaries who manage the trade for a specific cost.

All revenue for the services, net of overheads, would go to the members who control the platform and make the decisions. Trust is therefore not established with third parties but rather via encrypted consent enabled by intelligent encryption in transactions. This approach is often complex to understand and very far from the current technological system used in commerce, which could represent a problem for the diffusion of the Blockchain. However, international banks, investment firms, technology companies, and other stakeholders are investing significant capital and resources to evaluate Blockchain's benefits and potential impact.

The ability to execute transactions without the presence of an intermediary is well suited to a private market such as real estate and provides a viable alternative for exchanging building shares.

The ledger contains the history of a transaction, property, asset, or title; develops a secure digital identifier for each proposed transaction. Subsequently, Blockchain technology offers the possibility of transferring funds in new ways, for example, using an encrypted (or cryptographic) digital currency such as Bitcoin.

To summarize, Blockchain is arousing broad interest for businesses as:

– allows data protection through verification, consent process, encryption, and decentralization;

- it is transparent as the transactions are visible to all members of the network;
- reduces brokerage costs on transactions.

How Does It Work

One party participating in the transaction starts the process by creating a block, and all of them can form a data block. This block is verified and validated by thousands, perhaps millions, of computers distributed over the network and thus is added to the chain permanently. When one block is completed, another is generated, which gives rise to an exponential number of blocks (Fig. 2.10).

Blocks can be validated by the network using cryptographic means, which makes any attempt at fraud and forgery virtually impossible.

Each block contains a timestamp, the hash value of the previous block ("parent"), and a nonce, a random number to verify the hash. This mechanism guarantees the integrity of the entire Blockchain up to the first block ("genesis block"). The hash values are unique, enabling fraud to be effectively prevented. However, if most of the nodes in the network agree with the consensus mechanism on the validity of transactions in a given block and on the block itself, the latter can be added to the chain. Therefore, if it complies with the established rules, any additions to the ledger are automatically replicated in all its copies (Narayanan et al., 2016).

It follows that the keystone of the entire Blockchain technology is the so-called consensus mechanism, which guarantees that the information entered in the blocks is correct and consistent with the rules established in

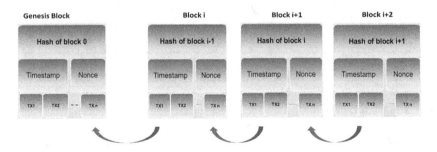

Fig. 2.10 How Blockchain technology works. Source: Authors' elaboration on reports by Zheng et al. (2016), "Blockchain Challenges and Opportunities: A Survey"

the protocol (Baliga, 2017; Swanson, 2015). Therefore, new transactions are not automatically added to the ledger. Instead, the consent process can be of two types:

1. Proof of Work: ensures that transactions are stored in a block for a specific time, for example, 10 min in the Bitcoin Blockchain, before being transferred to the ledger. To guarantee the authenticity of the information, all users have the right to vote (against payment of a price established upstream). The number of votes decides which transaction should or should not be included in the process. After that, the information in the Blockchain can no longer be changed. The disadvantages are given by: 51% risk of hacker attack (by subjects who have many voting rights), high energy consumption;
2. Proof of Stake: causes when a new block is added, the creator of the next block is automatically chosen. Manning (2016) argues that a proof-of-stake protocol will reduce the risk of a hacker attack by 51%. If someone were to have the computing power within a 51% protocol, they would also have to own, for example, 51% of total existing Bitcoins.

The Difference Between Public and Private Blockchains
The Blockchain was born as a public way to carry out transactions (these are the so-called unpermissioned or permissionless Blockchains that anyone can access). Still, currently, this technology is spreading (in areas other than cryptocurrencies) more and more within more or less closed ecosystems, with the consequent birth of private Blockchains called permissioned because they require a specific authorization to access them and which are often the result of the delivery of consortia for particular supply chains.

The governance model of the Blockchain can be classified according to two dimensions (Hilmena & Rauchs, 2017):

- "authorized/without authorization"
- "public/private"

The first dimension refers to the ability or not of the subject to participate in the consent mechanism. In contrast, the second refers to the possibility of a user being able to access Blockchain technology (Backlund, 2016). In particular:

- In an authorization-free Blockchain, anyone, including non-"secure" subjects, can participate in the consent of the processes. Therefore, anyone is free to be an active part of the network. The costs are higher, and the speed of transactions is slower than that recorded on an authorized chain;
- Authorized Blockchains are kept centralized on one (or more) authorized users. In this case, authorized users verify each transaction.

Finally, there are hybrid systems: open networks that operate on behalf of a community that shares a common interest, where access is limited to a small number of trusted users (e.g., Ripple).

On the other hand, regardless of the subject's ability or not to participate in the consensus mechanism in transactions, the Blockchain can be both public and private (Buterin, 2014):

- Anyone can join the network and use Blockchain technology in a public ecosystem. A user can access a specific service without the provider's authorization. In a public Blockchain without approval, there is no central authority. Anyone with an Internet connection can use the service, read the file and the transaction history, and participate in the consent mechanism. The consensus protocol is mandatorily based on cryptoeconomics because of the system's open nature and because it is impossible to presume trust between the "nodes." It is a system that works in the absence without the requirement of trust between users. Therefore, it is considered to be completely decentralized. For example, Bitcoin is a public ecosystem.
- In a private Blockchain, users are known and controlled. They will only be able to access the Blockchain service if the service provider allows them to do so. In doing so, participants are accountable for their actions and are therefore incentivized to behave honestly to avoid legal proceedings. Furthermore, transactions are verified by a limited number of nodes and are therefore faster and cheaper. Thus, the transaction fees are significantly lower than those charged for public networks (Fig. 2.11).

Also, in this case, there is a hybrid system called "consortium register." In the hybrid system, a couple of institutions predetermine and control

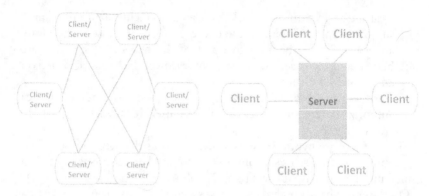

Fig. 2.11 Public (right) and private (left) Blockchain. Source: Authors' elaboration

the consensus protocol. For example, a consortium registry could have 20 institutions handling a node, and each new block added must be signed by at least 15 institutions to be considered valid. This system is considered partially decentralized, and the reading permissions could be open to the public or limited to participants.

Based on the two dimensions, it is, therefore, possible to identify four types of Blockchain governance models (Fig. 2.12).

Challenges and Criticalities of the Blockchain
The main obstacle to introducing Blockchain in enterprises is the lack of compatibility with existing systems, which would require a significant overhaul of the processes to ensure that Blockchain technology can be applied (Deloitte, 2018).

Another criticality concerns the lack of or limited regulation that the European Commission recently tried to address with a new set of rules and controls.

Furthermore, the issue of privacy is particularly complex. The main problem is that the Blockchain is, by its nature, an open and transparent system, and the information contained in the register can be consulted at any time by all network users. Suppose this represents one of the main strengths of Blockchain technology from the point of view of the immutability of information, on the other hand. In that case, it represents a conflict with the issue of privacy.

		Read	Write	Commit
Open	Public Permissionless	Open to Anyone	Anyone	Anyone
	Private Permissionless	Open to Anyone	Authorized Participants	Anyone
Closed	Public Permissionless	Restricted	Anyone	Authorized Participants
	Private Permissionless	Restricted	Network Only	Network Only

Fig. 2.12 The governance models of the Blockchain. Source: Authors' elaboration

It is, therefore, necessary to find a balance between transparency and control that many subjects seem to have identified in the permissioned Blockchain.

So what is needed so that the advantages brought about by the use of Blockchain technology can be appreciated by everyone? According to the Blockchain and Distributed Ledger Observatory of the Politecnico di Milano, many factors can contribute to the growth of this phenomenon:

1. The need for greater attention to existing and established Blockchain-based applications and solutions;
2. the entry into the field of prominent digital players such as Facebook, Amazon, and Alibaba in terms of innovation capacity and diffusion of the phenomenon;
3. a regulatory framework and standardization work that allows and encourages businesses to invest in the Blockchain;
4. the availability of KPIs, data, and scenarios makes it possibly better to evaluate the advantages, risks, and necessary resources.

2.4.2   The Application of the Blockchain to Real Estate

The Blockchain is a promising technology tool for all service categories in the real estate and home automation sectors.

Real estate transactions today generally require time, physical proximity, and relationships. This process takes time and is often inefficient. Crowston and Wigand (2010) argue that a real estate transaction usually occurs in five steps: listing, research, evaluation, negotiation, and execution which in turn includes about 33 passages according to Lantmäteriet and Chromaway (2016) (Fig. 2.13).

There are many subjects involved in a transaction: real estate agents, lawyers, surveyors, the land registry, banks for obtaining a loan, and so on. These have data that are public in themselves but are stored in private sites. To access the information he needs, a buyer must contact the authorized specialists to access the archives. Lantmäteriet and Chromaway (2016) argue that one of the main reasons it takes a long time to carry out a real estate transaction is the repeated process of validating the information. Many documents are signed on paper and must be sent via the postal service. Document validation must therefore be done through manual processes. Due to many signed copies, errors often occur that need to be corrected, causing a further increase in the time required to carry out a transaction and the costs incurred. Case and Shiller (1989) argue that one of the reasons that lead to the inefficiency of the real estate market is precisely caused by the sector's high transaction costs.

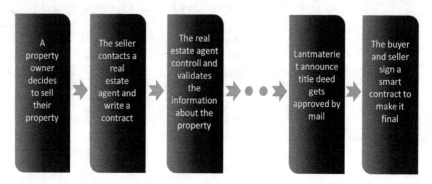

Fig. 2.13   The process of selling a property. Source: Authors' elaboration

Blockchain technology has the potential to revolutionize the entire contractual process currently used by eliminating a "human" intermediary (Peters & Panayi, 2015).

The Blockchain could make all information about real estate available almost instantly to all counterparties and, once the agreed commissions have been established and paid, proceed with the transaction. Furthermore, it is a much safer technology than today as fraud and loss of documents cannot occur or are minimized, and the whole transaction process could take much less time than it is today.

Therefore, we immediately notice the enormous savings in time and money that Blockchain technology can bring to the real estate sector.

However, there are many potential applications of the Blockchain to the real estate sector, and they refer to:

- leasing contracts agreed directly between lessor and lessee;
- purchase and/or disposal of land;
- availability of information regarding the transfer of ownership of a specific property (mainly crucial in the acquisition phase);
- historical data on building maintenance.

The benefits for the real estate sector are innumerable, starting from the Blockchain's ability to authenticate and track transactions in real-time without using a third party, such as a bank. All steps within a lease or sales agreement could be automated, while payments could be sent or received instantly, even outside business hours. This mechanism would also remove current barriers for investors, making assets more liquid and transparent.

Some governments (e.g., Dubai) are experimenting with using Blockchain in the land registry, hoping that digital recording of this information can reduce costs. Save time and increase security throughout the transaction.

Smart Contracts
Smart contracts had already been proposed in 1993, but the market was not ready to implement the technology in the various economic sectors (Omohundro, 2014).

Intelligent contracts are today defined as scripts stored on the Blockchain that generate automated processes in several stages (Christidis & Devetsikiotis, 2016).

They are platforms like that of Ethereum (a non-profit organization consisting of a decentralized platform running smart contracts) that hold a large amount of money and use an open network system to attract counterparties (Luu et al., 2016). Ethereum is one of the most established intelligent contract systems that use Bitcoin-like Blockchain technology, making it possible for complex contracts to be executed automatically and quickly (Omohundro, 2014).

Specifically, a smart contract is a digitally programmed contract that automatically executes its terms without the help of third parties once the contractual conditions are met. They can be defined as "automated and executable agreements" in which the clauses of an agreement between two or more parties are programmed through an alphanumeric code that provides a predefined set of instructions; the code is stored on the Blockchain just as transactions are typically stored on other control chains.

Unlike traditional contracts that offer the possibility to perform the services as established in the contract itself or to default and meet the relative consequences, this option is not available in a smart contract where the execution of the contract (e.g., payment) is automated, and the transaction is executed by default.

Rentberry decided to develop Blockchain-based intelligent contracts in the real estate sector and create a solution for the rental market.

In physical assets such as real estate, Rentberry's smart contracts perform the following functions:

- Allows both parties to sign the contract securely and digitally through the public and private key system on the Blockchain, without the help of institutional intermediaries;
- Automatically and securely pays the monthly rent on the agreed date and time, taking the sum established in the contract from the tenant's account and automatically paying it to the owner. Once the payment has been made, access to the apartment via Smart Lock will be extended for the following month, and vice versa, access will be denied;
- Keep the deposit within the smart contract. It will be the same digital contract that will then allow the owner to use it in case of damage or return it to the tenant;
- Allows the visit to the property to be scheduled through a particular smart contract that will provide access to the visitor via a personal private key enabled by the owner, but without the need for his physical presence.

To be operational, these technologies must first be enabled within the building by providing a Smart Lock Technology.

2.5   Market Analysis

There are several approaches to identifying areas of Proptech.
The Proptech classification derives mainly from the following criteria:

- Implemented technology, which can be distinguished in evolutionary phases such as Proptech 1.0, 2.0, and 3.0 (Baum, 2017);
- value chain or development process, divided into various phases such as pre-construction, construction, and post-construction (Maududy & Gamal, 2019);
- stakeholders involved, which can be grouped into retail, commercial, and residential (Shaw, 2018).

In January 2021, the total number of Proptech companies active in Europe (excluding the United Kingdom, which left the European community at the end of 2020) was 633 (Unissu, 2021).

In Table 2.4, we have reported, by country, the number of Proptech companies active in Europe, the respective percentage of the total (633) and the cumulative percentage.

Among the various Member States, some stand out for the number of companies present, such as France (148; 23.4% of the total), Germany (72; 11.4% of the total), and the Netherlands (69; 10.9% of the total). More generally, it can be observed that in the first five countries (France, Germany, the Netherlands, Finland, and Slovakia) there is more than 60% of the total number of Proptech and Contech companies active in Europe based on the classification present in the Unissu database, 2021.

In Italy, only 15 active companies represent 2.5% of the total of Member States—a number much lower than the importance of the Italian real estate sector in the European context.

Following the first classification criterion of companies active in the real estate sector (identified by Baum in 2017), we classified the proptech according to the evolutionary phase in which the company was founded (Fig. 2.14).

It is interesting to observe how it is possible to distinguish three different dynamics for the respective evolutionary phases of Proptech. In the first phase, which includes the period from 1980 to 1999, fewer than ten

Table 2.4   Number of Proptech companies active in Europe in 2021

	N° of companies	% of the total	% cumulative
France	148	23.4	23
Germany	72	11.4	35
Netherlands	69	10.9	46
Finland	59	9.3	55
Slovakia	59	9.3	64
Sweden	30	4.7	69
Spain	29	4.6	74
Denmark	23	3.6	77
Austria	20	3.2	80
Belgium	20	3.2	84
Ireland	16	2.5	86
Italy	15	2.4	88
Poland	14	2.2	91
Czech Republic	11	1.7	92
Hungary	11	1.7	94
Estonia	7	1.1	95
Slovenia	6	0.9	96
Portugal	5	0.8	97
Lithuania	4	0.6	98
Luxemburg	4	0.6	98
Greece	3	0.5	99
Cyprus	2	0.3	99
Latvia	2	0.3	99
Bulgaria	1	0.2	100
Croatia	1	0.2	100
Malta	1	0.2	100
Romania	1	0.2	100

Source: Authors' elaboration of Unissu 2021 data

Proptech companies have been established yearly. In the second phase, however, the number of companies based each year is between five and ten in the first five years 2000–2004, and then begins to grow and stabilize between ten and fifteen for the last four years 2004–2007 of the era of Proptech 2.0. On the other hand, the third evolutionary phase deserves a more detailed analysis. In fact, from 2008 to 2016, we can observe a net growth that varies from 20 companies (between 2008 and 2011) to over 80 in 2016. This trend could make us think of an exponential growth dynamic if we do not notice the subsequent abrupt relapse between 2017 and 2019, which we return to under the 20 companies established

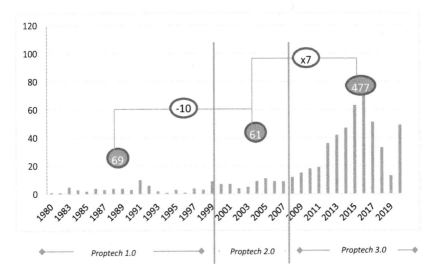

Fig. 2.14 Number of Proptech companies founded each year in Europe. Source: Authors' elaboration of Unissu 2021 data

annually. On the other hand, 2020 shows an activity level equal to 2014 and 2017, which makes us reflect on how the Proptech sector will further evolve from 2021 onward.

The second classification criterion, carried out based on the value chain, leads us to classify the companies by distinguishing between those that deal with the pre-construction and construction phase of the property from those specialized in the post-construction stage (Table 2.5).

About 67% of the Proptech companies that deal with managing the pre-construction and construction phase are located in France (29.7%), Germany (12.9%), the Netherlands (12.9%), and Finland (11.6%), while the remaining nations the percentage is always less than 4.3%. On the other hand, the presence of Proptech companies in Europe dealing with the post-construction phase is more proportionate, except in Slovakia, where the percentage of active companies is significant (26.3%).

Finally, according to the third criterion identified by Shaw in 2018, we classified the companies based on the stakeholders involved: retail, commercial, and residential, and on which we produced three distinct views.

From Fig. 2.15, it can be immediately observed that the retail sector occupies a minimal part (5%) of the focus of Proptech companies, while

Table 2.5 Classification of Proptech companies according to the value chain

Countries	% Contech	Countries	% Proptech
France	29.7	Slovakia	26.3
Germany	12.9	France	8.9
Netherland	12.9	Germany	7.9
Finland	11.6	Spain	7.4
Sweden	4.3	Netherland	6.3
Denmark	4.1	Sweden	5.8
Belgium	3.4	Austria	4.7
Spain	3.4	Czech Republic	4.7
Austria	2.5	Finland	4.2
Slovakia	2.0	Ireland	4.2
Ireland	1.8	Italy	3.7
Italy	1.8	Poland	3.7
Hungary	1.8	Belgium	2.6
Poland	1.6	Denmark	2.6
Slovenia	1.1	Estonia	1.6
Estonia	0.9	Hungary	1.6
Portugal	0.9	Greece	1.1
Lithuania	0.7	Croatia	0.5
Luxemburg	0.7	Lithuania	0.5
Cyprus	0.5	Luxemburg	0.5
Latvia	0.5	Portugal	0.5
Czech Republic	0.5	Slovenia	0.5
Greece	0.2	Bulgaria	0.0
Romania	0.2	Cyprus	0.0
Bulgaria	0.0	Latvia	0.0
Croatia	0.0	Malta	0.0
Malta	0.0	Romania	0.0

Source: Authors' elaboration of Unissu 2021 data

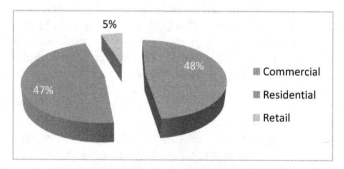

Fig. 2.15 Classification of Proptech companies by stakeholders involved. Source: Authors' elaboration of Unissu 2021 data

the companies active in the commercial and residential part share 95% of the market equally (48% and 47%, respectively).

Finally, we made a brief focus by country on the two main stakeholder categories (commercial and residential). Comparing the two distributions (Fig. 2.16) with Table 2.4 above, it can be observed that there is no substantial geographical difference between the distribution of the total number of Proptech companies and the classification by stakeholder. In fact, among the top 3 countries for the number of active companies (France, Germany, the Netherlands, Finland, Slovakia), France and Germany remain on the podium, while the Netherlands, Finland, and Slovakia alternate the first places between the commercial and residential sectors.

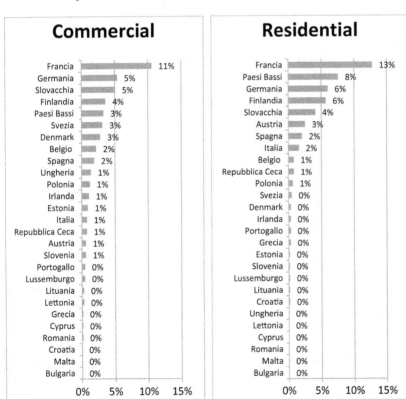

Fig. 2.16 Focus by country on the distribution of companies operating in the commercial and residential sectors. Source: Authors' elaboration of Unissu 2021 data

Another necessary consideration is the concentration of the market, which remains strong in the top five players but is undoubtedly more significant in the case of the residential than the commercial.

2.6   Conclusion

As with many other industries, technology is starting to affect traditional real estate operations. Technology introduction generally creates efficiency in the process through automation and uniformity. It is being implemented through Proptech in the real estate sector after years of underinvestment.

These new technologies bring many benefits to consumers and market players if they can exploit them to their advantage.

This chapter has explored the theme of technological innovation in the real estate sector, particularly the phenomenon called Proptech, focusing on the phenomenon's evolution over the years, the resulting advantages and disadvantages, and the new business models companies are trying to implement. To innovate the real estate sector characterized by a high level of static and finally touched on the topic of Blockchain applied to Proptech.

After analyzing the most historical and evolutionary part of the phenomenon, we proceeded with an initial analysis aimed at elucidating the advantages and pitfalls of implementing new digital strategies in the sector. The main benefits include reducing investment risks, improving customer engagement and satisfaction, better budget management, more detailed and less biased valuations, better property utilization, urban planning transactions, and the advent of smart contracts. On the other hand, the leading players are facing the problem of the complex implementation of these innovations linked to possible issues in terms of data privacy; quality, standardization.

Among the opportunities identified we have highlighted: the different resolution of judicial conflicts on the properties, the performance forecast for the first phases of the real estate project, the social network services for contact with investors or buyers that allow the property to be viewed even remotely, the hybrid models of real estate agencies encouraged by a reduction in fixed costs on personnel and better customer management, thanks to the in-depth knowledge of users following the high amount of data they have available through technology, the crowdfunding market that allows finance the property more quickly, and, obviously, the subject of Blockchain technology applied to real estate.

However, it is unclear how these fields will evolve; it all depends on their acceptance of the market and continuous improvement to satisfy stakeholders' requests.

REFERENCES

Aalbers, M., & Haila, A. K. E. (2018). The financialization of housing: A political economy approach. *Urban Studies, 55*(15), 1821–1835.

Alfaraj, Q. (2019). Attaining and sustaining competitive advantage in Dubai's real estate industry.

Backlund, L. (2016). *A technical overview of distributed ledger technologies in the Nordic capital market.* Uppsala University. http://diva-portal.org.

Baliga, A., (2017, April). *Understanding blockchain consensus models.*

Baum, A. (2017). *PropTech 3.0: The future of real estate.* Said Business School. http://eureka.sbs.ox.ac.uk/6485/1/122037%20PropTech_FINAL.pdf.

Brynjolfsson, E., & Mitchell, T. (2017). What can machine learning do? Workforce implications. *Science, 358*(6370), 1530–1534. https://doi.org/10.1126/science.aap8062

Bughin, J., & Van Zeebroeck, N. (2017). The best response to digital disruption. *MIT Sloan Management Review, 58*(4), 80–86.

Buterin, V. (2014). *A next-generation smart contract and decentralized application platform.* White Paper.

Case, K. E., & Shiller, R. J. (1989). The efficiency of the market for single-family homes. *American Economic Review, 79*(1), 125–137.

Chircu, A. M., & Kauffman, R. J. (2000). Limits to value in electronic commerce-related IT investments. *Journal of Management Information Systems, 17*(2), 59–80.

Choi, J., Kaul, K., & Goodman, L. (2019). *FinTech innovation in the home purchase and financing market.* Urban Institute.

Christidis, K., & Devetsikiotis, M. (2016). Blockchains and smart contracts for the internet of things. *IEEE Access, 4*, 2292–2303. http://ieeexplore.ieee.org/

Coffman, K. G., & Odlyzko, A. M. (2001, July). The size and growth rate of the internet. *Optical Fiber Telecommunications IV Journal.*

Conway, C. (2019). Search engine to service engine. *Property Journal*, 58–59.

Crowston, K., & Wigand, R. T. (2010). Real estate war in cyberspace: An emerging electronic market? *International Journal of Electronic Markets, 9*, 37–44.

Dawson, S. (2016). Technology: The power of the cloud. *Journal Real Estate Institute of New South Wales, 67*(2), 35.

Deloitte. (2018). *Building the future. Real estate predictions.* https://www2.deloitte.com/content/dam/Deloitte/global/Documents/About-Deloitte/gx-real-estate-predictions-2018-report.pdf.

Devaney, S., Livingstone, N., McAllister, P., & Nanda, A. (2017). Institutional convergence in real estate markets: A comparative study of brokerage models and transaction costs. *Journal of Real Estate Literature, 25*(1), 169–188.

Forbes. (2018). *3.0 PropTech investors talk trends, game-changers and the future of real estate.* https://www.forbes.com/sites/alyyale/2018/09/13/3-proptech-investors-talk-trends-game-changers-the-future-of-real-estate/#45aa9a591812.

Forman, C., Goldfarb, A., & Greenstein, S. (2018). *How geography shapes-and is shaped by-the internet* (The New Oxford Handbook of Economic Geography). Oxford University Press.

Fuster, A., Plosser, M., Schnabl, P., & Vickery, J. (2019). The role of technology in mortgage lending. *The Review of Financial Studies, 32*(5), 1854–1899.

Gee, H. (2010). Residential real estate data on the internet: Benefits and limits. *Journal of Business and Finance Librarianship, 15*(2), 104–122.

Gibilaro L. (2016). I principali player internazionali. L'evoluzione delle piatta-forme peer-to-peer. In Filotto U. (Ed.), *Il peer to peer lending: mito o realtà?*, Bancaria Editrice, Roma.

Hilmena G., & Rauchs M. (2017) Global blockchain benchmarking study. Accessed September 01, 2022, from https://www.jbs.cam.ac.uk/.

ING. (2018). *Technology in the real estate sector.* Online. https://think.ing.com/uploads/reports/ING_EBZ_PropTech-Technlogy_in_the_real_estate_sector-June_2018_tcm162-148619.pdf

KPMG. (2018). The road to opportunity. A annual review of the real estate industry's journey into the digital age. https://assets.kpmg/.

Kuzma, J., O'Sullivan, S., Philippe, T. W., Koehler, J. W., & Coronel, R. S. (2017). Commercialization strategy in managing online presence in the unmanned aerial vehicle industry. *International Journal of Business Strategy, 17*(1), 59–68.

Lantmäteriet, T., & Chromaway, K. (2016). *Framtidens husköp I blockkedjan.* https://www.lantmateriet.se

Law, R., Leung, R., Lo, A., Leung, D., & Fong, L. H. N. (2015). Distribution channel in hospitality and tourism: Revisiting disintermediation from the perspectives of hotels and travel agencies. *International Journal of Contemporary Hospitality Management, 27*(3), 431–452.

Li, X., Li, Y., Liu, T., Qiu, J., & Wang, F. (2009). The method and tool of cost analysis for cloud computing. In *2009 IEEE International Conference on Cloud Computing* (pp. 93–100).

Littlefield, J. E., Bao, Y., & Cook, D. L. (2000). Internet real estate information: Are home purchasers are paying attention to it. *Journal of Consumer Marketing, 17*(7), 575–590.

Luu, L., Chu, D. H., Olickel, H., Saxena, P., & Hobor, A. (2016). *Making smart contracts smarter.* Retrieved March 9, 2017, from http://dl.acm.org

Manning, J. (2016). *Proof-of-work vs. proof-of-stake.* https://www.ethnews.com.

Mathew, P. A., Dunn, L. N., Sohn, M. D., Mercado, A., Custudio, C., & Walter, T. (2015). Big-data for building energy performance: Lessons from assembling a very large national database of building energy use. *Applied Energy, 140*, 85–93.

Maududy, C. F., & Gamal, A. (2019). Literature review: Technologies and property development. *IOP Conference Series: Earth and Environmental Science, 396*(1), https://doi.org/10.1088/1755-1315/396/1/012020.

Moore, F. (2018). What are iBuyers and are they a threat? *REIQ Journal,* 14.

Morabito, V. (2017). *Business innovation through blockchain.* Springer International Publishing.

Narayanan, A., Bonneau, J., Felten, E., Miller, A., & Goldfeder, S. (2016). *Bitcoin and cryptocurrency technologies: A comprehensive introduction.* Princeton University Press.

Ojo, B., Oyetunji, B. O., & Oyetunji, A. K. (2018). Barriers to ICT deployment in the Nigerian real estate. *Journal of Science and Technology, 4*(2), 57–65.

Omohundro, S. (2014). Cryptocurrencies, smart contracts, and artificial intelligence. *AI Matters, 1*(2), 19–21. http://dl.acm.org

Peters, G. W., & Panayi, E. (2015). *Understanding modern banking ledgers through blockchain technologies: Future of transaction processing and smart contracts on the internet of money.* https://link.springer.com/.

Read, W. (2019). *The evolution of dirt: Real estate in the age of disruption.* Plan II Honors Theses-Openly Available.

RICS. (2017). *RICS valuation – Global Standards 2017.* Routledge.

Shaw, J. (2018). Platform Real Estate: Theory and practice of new urban real estate markets. *Urban Geography*, 1–28.

Swanson, T. (2015). *Consensus-as-a-service: A brief report on the emergence of permissioned.* Distributed ledger systems. Work Paper.

Ullah, F., Sepasgozar, S. M., & Wang, C. (2018). A systematic review of smart real estate technology: Drivers of, and barriers to, the use of digital disruptive technologies and online platforms. *Sustainability, 10*(9), 3142.

Unissu. (2021). PropTech in Italy: Everything you need to know 2021. Accessed September 01, 2022, from https://www.unissu.com/.

Venture Scanner. (2016). *Real estate technology.* Q2 update in 15 visuals.

Walport, M. (2016). *Distributed ledger technology: Beyond blockchain.* UK Government Office for Science.

Wessels, P. (2016). *Blockchain will have an enormous impact on the real estate sector.* PropertyNL.

Yasav, S. (2015). The impact of digital technology on consumer purchase behavior. *Journal of Financial Perspectives, 3*(3).

Zheng, Z., Xie, S., Dai, H. N., & Wang, H. (2016). Blockchain challenges and opportunities: A survey. *International Journal of Web and Grid Services, 14*(4). https://doi.org/10.1504/IJWGS.2018.095647

Zumpano, L. V., Johnson, K. H., & Anderson, R. I. (2003). Internet use and real estate brokerage market intermediation. *Journal of Housing Economics, 12*(2), 134–150.

CHAPTER 3

Real Estate Management IT Tools

Abstract Real estate investment requires time managing the assets owned to maximize achieved results. Real estate management activities are based on the information collected, professionals and companies that can help manage the asset, and the medium- and long-term strategy defined for each asset owned.

This chapter focused on proptech's services that can be requested for both transaction-intensive and Judgment-intensive projects. It will also evaluate the support provided in constructing the medium- and long-term investment strategy for the portfolio of assets owned.

Keywords Real estate risk • Risk management • Transaction-intensive • Judgment-intensive • Strategy

3.1 Introduction

The real estate market has traditionally not been inclined to new technologies that can change business models and real estate investment management approaches and is very traditional in identifying business best practices. The evolution in recent years has led not only to the emergence of so-called smart cities but also to the smart spaces and buildings that are now the assets demanded by the market and that developers and investors must identify in the market to be successful in real estate (Lecomte, 2020).

G. Mattarocci, X. Scimone, *The New Era of Real Estate*, https://doi.org/10.1007/978-3-031-16731-7_3

The main benefits of technology applied to the real estate sector are related to the solutions available for offering user services, managing and monitoring the relationship between owner, user, and investor, designing and monitoring a building, and reducing the environmental impact related to the development and use of the property (Bröchner et al., 2019).

Nowadays, proptech represents a no-longer-deferred solution for real estate operators destined to spread to all activities related to property management that can benefit from the potential offered by technology (Starr et al., 2020). The services provided by proptech companies represent an innovative solution that has changed the operating model of major players active in real estate management to take advantage of the opportunities offered by technology and present more effective forms of minimizing the risks that characterize different types of real estate investments.

The chapter will analyze proptech services offered for property management, focusing on data and experiences related to the European reality. Section 3.2 will examine the individual risks that characterize real estate investment by distinguishing the sources of risk affecting the development of real estate investments (Sect. 3.2.1) versus income properties (Sect. 3.2.2). Section 3.3 is devoted to an analysis of the solutions offered by proptech by distinguishing services intended for its ongoing use by the owner (Sect. 3.2.2), activities that require the processing of an extensive set of information (Sect. 3.2.2), and one-time intervention that can be carried out by the property owner (Sect. 3.3.3).

3.2   Real Estate Risk

Risk factors associated with real estate investment change significantly depending on the object, and it is possible to identify some macro-categories of real estate that are characterized by relevant risk factors of different nature (Plattner, 1988):

- land with or without construction permits;
- residential;
- commercial

Investment in land represents the investment with the highest risk profile for the investor because the transaction's success depends on urban planning, architectural, engineering, and economic profiles. In this case, technical and financial due diligence represents the most critical profiles for the operation's success, and the timing of completion and marketing of the work cannot be estimated ex-ante except with a high degree of approximation.

Investment in residential projects usually has a low-risk profile. It represents an attractive opportunity even for non-professional operators who want to pursue results in the medium to long term. The main aspects to consider when assessing the risk of the transaction are related to the liquidity of the rental and property market, which in some areas and for some types of properties can be a potential problem for the investor.

Commercial properties (stores, offices, hotels, warehouses, factories, etc...) are a complex asset to evaluate whose performance depends on general economic trends, the tenant's business sector, the modularity of the property, and its location. Assessing the riskiness of such investments uses similar approaches to the residential segment, but the level of complexity of the data to be collected is much higher given that the market is less liquid and characterized by greater specialization of buyers and sellers.

The following section will examine the risks involved in greenfield and brownfield projects (Sect. 3.2.1) and income-producing properties (Sect. 3.2.2).

3.2.1 Greenfield and Brownfield Projects

In the case of real estate development or redevelopment projects, the investor engages in a business activity whose object is the purchase of building or brownfield land, the making of investments aimed at increasing the value of the properties in the portfolio and creating the conditions for obtaining a capital gain from the sale of the asset (Hettenhouse & Dee, 1976).

The risk assumed for the realization of the project is for such properties related to the magnitude of outflows generated by the investment, the time required for inflows to occur, and the various external factors that may result in unexpected costs and/or delays and the risks associated with the variability of the market value of properties in the area (Flanagan & Norman, 2003). Development or redevelopment involves the developer's interaction with various public and private counterparts (Gehner, 2008) (Fig. 3.1).

The market characteristics of the area or property to be redeveloped determine the initial price associated with the start of the redevelopment project and, consequently, the profit margins on the operation.

Fig. 3.1 Parties involved in greenfield and brownfield projects. Source: Authors' elaboration

The local government sets the rules for the redevelopment operation and is one of the main counterparts with whom the investor must interact throughout the investment project.

To assess the overall risk of a real estate development or redevelopment operation and the role of each counterparty with whom the real estate developer must interact, the overall project is usually distinguished into the following intervention phases:

– Identification of the area or property;
– Design of the intervention;
– Management of the project;
– Decommissioning of the property.

Identifying the area of intervention (greenfield or brownfield) presupposes a study of current and prospective demand to define an appropriate price for the asset acquisition about the prospects of renting or selling the property that will be built. The evaluation to be carried out must consider the value of the area, the type of intervention to be carried out, the forms of financing available, and the time required to complete the intervention, and compare these profiles with other investment opportunities available in the market to select the projects with the most significant potential (D'Arcy & Keogh, 2002). The parties involved in this process stage are the seller of the area or property to be redeveloped, the technical consultant who must perform legal and urban planning due diligence on the project, and the local government. The risks associated with this phase are related to the regulatory and urban planning profiles that need to be examined in detail by the investor and the risks related to forecasting market demand for the type of property that will be built.

The planning phase considers not only the technical profiles related to the structure's definition but also the intervention's economic sustainability based on the costs associated with the project and the prospects for renting and selling the type of property built (Barkham, 2002). The planning of the intervention must pay particular attention to the layout and organization of the property's space in such a way as to make the investment attractive and economically viable for the potential buyer based on the current and prospective space requirements for the user to whom the property will be offered for sale (Huffman, 2002). The assessment considers the contemporary characteristics of the market and the potential supply that is expected to be realized before the completion of the project, expected interventions on the location that may change its desirability in the market, the technical characteristics of the property, and its degree of flexibility to adapt to any specific requirements of the potential buyer or tenant, and the value and relevance of comparable properties in the area. The analysis that is carried out makes it possible to identify the strengths and weaknesses of the intervention, allowing variants to the project to be evaluated as well, which can potentially increase the profit margin associated with the completion of the project. The developer interacts in this phase with technical consultants who support him in assessing the economic and technical feasibility of the project, with local governments for related permits, and with the capital market to identify possible investors or lenders interested in participating in the project. The risks associated with this second phase of the project are particularly relevant because the developer has incurred the costs of acquiring the land or the building to be redeveloped, will need to cover all costs associated with site planning, will need to identify appropriate forms of financing, and will need to adapt the project to the risks and unexpected events that may arise depending on the characteristics of the intervention area and the permitting process.

The project management phase involves starting the construction site by identifying suppliers and subcontractors and negotiating with each of them the economic and technical terms of their contribution to the project's success. At this stage, the gift of engineers is limited to construction management unless there is a need to modify the project during construction. Still, the developer needs to interact frequently with the capital market to cover needs related to the operation. Managing this phase requires the input of experts who can do detailed due diligence on each contract that ensures that measurable commitments are established for each counterparty involved and minimizes the risk of litigation during the life of the construction site. The success of the development operation and profitability for the developer are linked to the ability to minimize the time associated with completing the process to limit the time horizon over which the investment absorbs resources. The cost and time associated with the operation will vary depending on the type of project, given that greenfield projects are usually in non-densely populated areas with no significant constraints in terms of the type and size of the development. In contrast, brownfield operations often involve essential and historic sites of the city and are subject to more excellent controls and constraints during the construction phase (i.a., Cerasoli & Mattarocci, 2021). A frequently used solution to partially reduce the burdens associated with financing the construction site and the risks associated with demand uncertainty involves directly engaging the property market before the completion of the construction site to assess the possibility of selling part of the property on paper by granting buyers a discount from the average market price for the already completed property (Li & Chau, 2019).

The final phase of the construction site involves planning and managing the disposal of the property through sale or lease to a third party. This phase should be initiated before the construction site closes so there is sufficient time to implement an effective strategy based on market demand. The last stage of the real estate development or redevelopment project involves much interaction with the rental and property market to identify the final buyer or tenant of the property, and this phase often requires the support of legal counsel for contracting and agents/brokers to minimize the time on the market for the property. Time management in the final phase of the development project assumes proper planning and control of all stages of the construction site to avoid delays concerning the progress of the work.

3.2.2   Income-Producing Projects

The management of income-producing properties involves the interaction of the investor with various public and private counterparts (Gehner, 2008) (Fig. 3.2).

In the case of income properties, the risk assessment must consider the risk associated with existing contracts, if any, based on contract specifications compared to the market average and on the expected effects when the existing agreements are concluded. The main risks that characterize investments in income properties can be traced to:

- Displacement risks;
- Risks of tenant default;
- Risks related to the management of the property;
- Sale and relocation risks.

Fig. 3.2 Parties involved in greenfield and brownfield projects. Source: Authors' elaboration

Investing in income properties requires identifying tenants who can lease the property on medium- to long-term leases and minimizing the percentage of properties owned by the investor. The vacancy rate (vacancy rate) depends on the rent charged by the landlord and the affordability of the proposed rent of potential tenants (Gabriel & Nothaft, 1988). The level of equilibrium in the medium to long term for the vacancy rate depends mainly on the supply (current and prospective) of properties with similar characteristics, the benefits accruing to the individual tenant from the use of the property, and the cost and amount of financial resources required for the tenant to purchase a property if any (McDonald, 2000). The rent, however, may not be perfectly elastic concerning trends in supply and demand (Wheaton & Torto, 1998), and failure to revise the amount charged in line with new market conditions can have significant impacts on the size and number of vacancies (Hess & Liang, 2003). Such imperfections in the real estate market can result in longer or shorter time frames for identifying a new landlord (Haurin, 1988). The time it takes to lease previously vacant properties depends on the specific characteristics of the area in which the property is located (Gabriel & Nothaft, 2001) and the type of property (Wincott, 1997), and the features of the counterparty search process (Crockett, 1982).

A property owner, to obtain the most significant profit from the indirect use of the real estate he owns, must assess the likelihood that the occurrence of external events beyond his direct control will affect his ability to honor his commitments to the tenants to whom he has sold the property and, consequently, the number of inflows from the lease (Short et al., 2003). The assessment of this probability of default is carried out using different methodologies depending on the characteristics of the tenants distinguishing between the approaches for assessing household and corporate counterparties. In the case of households, the study of the probability of tenant insolvency is usually carried out by considering disposable income for the household as the primary variable (Sullivan & Fisher, 1988) and assuming that expenditure on housing represents the immediate need for the household that has priority over other possible expenditures (Ling, 1994). In the case of firms, the analysis must consider the amount of rent relative to turnover and assess differences in the rent charged relative to the rest of the areas of the country for the same type of property (Mueller, 1999).

The landlord of the property over the life of the investment bears the costs associated with extraordinary maintenance of the property and, in the case of vacant properties, the costs of routine maintenance. Regular maintenance costs are proportional to the property's size and the building's structural characteristics. It is higher for properties built with outdated technologies and has had extraordinary maintenance work done for many years (Springer & Waller, 1996).

When selling the property, the investor has to consider the costs associated with complying with the formal requirements in the individual country, which can have significant effects on the overall income result of the investment, and there are substantial differences in the magnitude of costs depending on the market considered. The main items to be considered are:

- Registration costs
- Agency fees
- Legal costs
- Taxation

Registration costs are related to the registration of the purchase and sale agreement and are payable to the local government for the registration of the new owner entity in the real estate registry and may vary depending on whether the buyer of the property is an individual or a company.

Agency fees are payable to the intermediary following the sale and are defined according to the property's value. The fees charged may differ from country to country and, within the country, depending on the characteristics of the town (smaller towns vs. large cities).

Legal costs are a function of the complexity of the transaction. They can range from the price associated with drafting the notarial deed (in countries where such activity is provided) to the costs associated with actual legal, due diligence.

Taxation on the negotiation of real estate can also be applied in some countries at the recording of the deed. Often, the rate charged depends not only on the property but also on the use of the property. Usually, taxation can be particularly concessional in the case of residential properties intended as first homes.

To measure transaction costs related to real estate investment, it is necessary to consider the amount paid at the property purchase and disposal stages, considering the specifics of the legislation applied in the individual country. The most frequently used proxy represented the overall average cost related to the purchase and disposal stage (roundtrip) (Table 3.1).

Table 3.1 The average cost of real estate trades in EU28 countries

Country	Average roundtrip fee	Country	Average roundtrip fee
Austria	11.20%	Italy	16.13%
Belgium	19.22%	Latvia	6.11%
Bulgaria	7.95%	Lithuania	3.44%
Czech Republic	8.77%	Luxembourg	14.31%
Cyprus	10.23%	Malta	18.56%
Croatia	10.53%	Netherlands	8.25%
Denmark	2.23%	Poland	6.73%
Estonia	4.08%	Portugal	12.92%
Finland	6.99%	Romania	11.82%
France	18.35%	Slovakia	5.81%
Germany	12.71%	Slovenia	6.35%
Greece	8.84%	Spain	11.09%
Hungary	10.65%	Sweden	8.25%
Ireland	9.07%	United Kingdom	10.03%

Source: Authors' elaboration on data provided by www.globalpropertyguide.com

The roundtrip fee includes the legal fees, the property ownership tax, the registration duty, notary fees, and the real estate agent fee. It has the cost for the seller and the buyer in the real estate transaction.

The average cost associated with roundtrip fees ranges from a low of 2.23% in Denmark to a high of 19.22 in France. The amount of expenditure incurred depends mainly on the degree of state intervention in individual transactions and the level of competition. European countries historically characterized by strong regulation in economic sectors (such as Belgium, France, and Italy) are represented by high outlays related to investment taxation. At the same time, other markets use the leverage of low tax to attract real estate investment even from foreign operators (Estonia, Lithuania, Poland, Slovakia, and Slovenia).

3.3   Risk Management Tools

Risk management solutions offered by Proptech companies can be reclassified according to the type of decision-making process that may affect the firm by distinguishing activities in (Battisti et al., 2020):

- Routine operations intended to be repeated frequently during the life of the project (Transaction-Intensive Processing);

- Interventions that require the collection and processing of a significant volume of information necessary for each business choice (Judgment-Intensive Processes);
- Interventions of an extraordinary nature require the definition of innovative strategies (Design and Strategy Support Processes).

The remainder of this paragraph will analyze the individual types of services developed through technology and big data to make managing types of real estate investments more efficient and effective.

In the remainder of the paragraph, the different categories of activities will be examined in detail, and the role of proptech tools in supporting each decision-making level will be highlighted.

3.3.1 Transaction-Intensive Processing

Owning a property implies significant maintenance costs throughout the life of the project. Solutions related to the Internet of Things (IoT) make it possible to use technology to minimize costs associated with management and, in some cases, anticipate major interventions, avoiding damage to the property and, consequently, reducing the overall cost of the operation (Kejriwal & Mahajan, 2016). Automated monitoring tools allow monitoring of consumption and the state of use of all elements that make up the property and can also be used to plan everyday activities, interventions, and calls for technicians whenever new problems are detected in the property (Kim, 2019). Data analysis on IoT properties has also shown that materials' consumption and wear and tear are minimized. Thus from the perspective of the owner and tenant, the choice to use this type of technology can allow maintenance work to be deferred over time. The most innovative tools for property management involve the continuous collection of data and automated decision-making tools for routine and ongoing building management choices (Lecomte, 2019). During the pandemic, due to constraints on the mobility of individuals and different needs for property use, there has been an increase in the use of automation tools that allow not only better enjoyment of the property but also create an up-to-date database with the behaviors of individual users of a property unit (Maalsen & Dowling, 2020). The services that proptech companies offer can enable more efficient and secure property management by collecting information through IoT tools that can minimize some of the costs associated with management (Fig. 3.3).

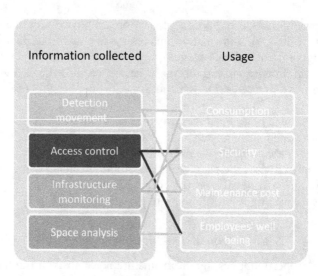

Fig. 3.3 Monitoring services offered by proptech companies. Source: Authors' elaboration

IoT services that allow monitoring the presence of people in different areas of the building make it possible to rationalize consumption related to utilities (electricity, water, etc...), and systems allow the collection of data on the use of the facility that the property owner can use to plan a better service offer toward users (occupancy rate of respective areas by time slots, no. of users present at the same time, etc...). External access control to the property impacts the facility's security and costs for security services and insurance while intern. In contrast, all access control can be used to limit the mobility of facility users to only certain areas of the property. The control and monitoring of facilities is a relevant variable for the company to carry out timely maintenance work where necessary and avoid waste and excessive consumption related to their incorrect operation. Room monitoring allows the detection of data such as air quality, humidity level, indoor temperature, etc., representing a valuable information source to monitor workers' quality of life and reduce consumption.

In the case of income properties, managing a large and heterogeneous tenant portfolio can create problems for the property owner. It may not be economically viable due to the high costs and time devoted to customer management. Solutions offered by the application of Blockchain enable the development of protocols for online contract signing and rent collection (Karamitsos et al., 2018).

Proptech solutions for property management were considered in the first instance for residential properties for which it was possible to realize temporary leases of facilities (e.g., AirB&B) that offered services to advertise even short-term rentals of residential units—requiring a commission from the landlord according to the rental price and the number of days rented in the relevant month and a commission from the user in proportion to the price paid for the accommodation (Guttentag, 2019). The provision of such a service assumes several external actors are involved in increasing the increasing quality of service perceived by the tenant and landlord (Fig. 3.4).

The tenant's interest is to have a standard of service comparable to that of the hotel industry for the same price range. It is, therefore, necessary to ensure adequate quality standards concerning the customer's expectations by using professionals who can provide maintenance work when required (property management) and room cleaning and sanitizing services when

Fig. 3.4 Counterparties involved in short-term rental of residential assets. Source: Authors' elaboration

the unit is to be rented to a new customer (facility management). The central aspect that motivates tenants to rent their property through these portals is the possibility of increasing their clientele and not having to manage the rent collection process themselves, avoiding all the problems associated with this profile. The proptech company must offer a certification and payment tracking service that minimizes the risk of fraud related to the individual rental contract entered into.

In recent years, shared use models of commercial real estate such as co-working spaces have developed that allow, especially for large properties, to find tenants whom pro-tempore can rent part of the facility. As of 2019, there were more than 19,400 co-working locations on a global scale, with a greater weight of the number of facilities offered in American, Asian, and European countries (Fig. 3.5).

The decision to use the property to offer shared space implies a significant increase in the number of counterparts with whom the owner must interact. Therefore, it may be essential to use automated tools for managing reservations, and billing based on the service used (desks, individual offices, meeting rooms, etc...). The subscription model subscribed to (monthly flat rates, daily rate, etc...). The business model initially created to meet demand from small companies and start-ups is destined to change

Fig. 3.5 Supply of co-working spaces on a worldwide scale. Source: Authors' elaboration on data provided by www.coworkingresources.org

over time as a function of the experience gained by companies during the health emergency that has led them to reevaluate flexible work models characterized by allowing part of the work to be done remotely in smart working mode. The new organization of work makes it convenient in many cases even for large companies to rethink their investment in real estate and to favor the use of co-working spaces to more flexibly and less expensively manage the costs associated with tangible assets and, in some cases, to be able to offer their employees logistical solutions that allow them to minimize the cost and time of travel to the workplace and improve the quality of the worker's view (e.g., proximity offices) (JLL, 2021).

3.3.2   Judgment-Intensive Processes

The design phase of building interventions involves identifying practical solutions to meet the end user's needs, and technological development has significantly changed the decision-making process related to such interventions. The first technical innovations associated with the possibility of carrying out integrated activities between different actors (owner, user, technical consultant, developer, lender, etc...) are related to the application of Building Information Modeling (BIM) models that allow jointly managing information related to technical standards, time and cost of the interventions to be carried out on the property (Wilkinson & Jupp, 2016) (Fig. 3.6).

The first 3 phases of the project are related to the technical feasibility of the intervention and allow for the construction of a detailed 3D design that reflects the needs of the end user and the stakeholders involved in the intervention phase. The subsequent three steps consider the time factor related to the interventions to be carried out, starting with a timeline (4) and arriving at detailed planning of activities (5) to build a complicated project that allows the progress of the work to be operationally verified. The final stages of the project include the cost profile (7), evaluating the economic effects of the choices made (8), and allowing for ongoing monitoring and management of the intervention on the property (9). The software used for project management has compatibility limitations that do not allow the full benefits of shared work to be exploited. The proptech solutions launched on the market allow the synergies associated with them to be controlled independently of the software usually used to manage the individual stages of the process (Lai et al., Lai et al., 2019).

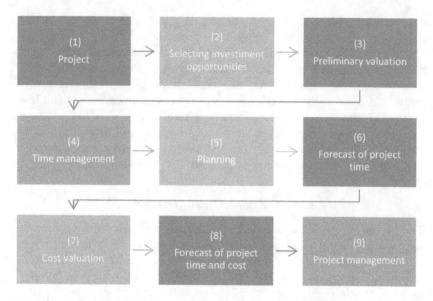

Fig. 3.6 BIM and real estate management. Source: Authors' elaboration

The management of a real estate development site (greenfield or brownfield) involves several actors with specific skills related to the direction of the property that needs to be coordinated during the project's life. Proptech solutions can contribute to the success of the real estate operation by facilitating and speeding up the exchange of information between the different actors and enabling more effective monitoring of the intervention and timely management of any critical issues (Roulac, 2019).

Maintenance interventions on the property often require significant time and costs for the property owner, and online tools can enable the management of such interventions to be optimized. Popular applications allow reporting via an online form of the fault by attaching photos that will help pre-assess the extent and type of damage and select the technician to be sent to the property for intervention. Such tools are also usually complemented by online tutorials that allow avoiding intervention by the technician in the case of minor issues and provide the tenant with all the necessary guidance to solve the problem themselves (Fields, 2022).

3.3.3   Design and Strategy Support Processes

Strategic decisions presuppose the availability of data to read the context and predict the effects of individual choices. Big data is vital for enriching the information assets based on decision findings. The minimum requirements must be met to create an appropriate decision-making tool are related to the three Vs. (McAfee & Brynjolfsson, 2012):

– Volume;
– Speed;
– Variety.

The information set to be collected for evaluating real estate investments is extensive because the evaluation of prices and rents cannot be separated from data on the area and technical characteristics of the building.

Real estate decisions are complex processes that take several weeks to complete. Still, information must be made available quickly, updated in real time, and presented in a format that the final decision maker quickly interprets.

The variety of sources used determines not only different formats of data collection and storage but also not comparable the frequency of observation from annual, yearly, or higher data (macro-economic information, censuses, etc...) to daily or lower frequency data (individual transactions, Internet listings, etc.).

IoT has offered the opportunity to manage the information database available using computers and automated systems, and nowadays, real estate is considered a data-driven market. The weight of nontraditional information on investment or rental decisions has increased in recent years, and it has modified the role of different types of information in pricing (McKinsey, 2018) (Fig. 3.7).

Traditional information considered in any real estate valuation model, such as the location and market, the performance of the particular type of property, and the specific characteristics of the asset, weighs less than 45% of the property's value. In comparison, qualitative information about the area's points of interest and their concentration relative to other locations contribute more than 55% to the asset's overall value.

The opportunities associated with the use of big data analytics and artificial intelligence tools to collect nontraditional data are significant and

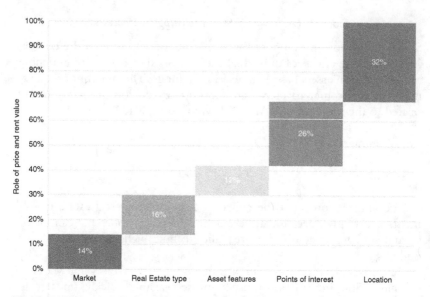

Fig. 3.7 The role of information on real estate values. Source: Authors' elaboration on McKinsey's (2018) survey data

allow for the integration of up-to-date real-time databases on the supply and demand for real estate in an area with contextual economic and social information (e.g., occupancy level, crime rate, etc...) that can change the future outlook for the size of interest (Worzala et al., 2021).

The operating model of such data analysis tools may be a classic black box in which the end user is unable to intervene in the organization of the information collected and the weight to be given to different information sources, or it may involve the end user's ability to customize the final report by selecting the definitive information to be presented or by changing the weight assigned by the system to some information over others (DeLisle et al., 2020).

In addition, Blockchain can be a helpful resource in the data collection phase necessary for investment or rental decisions because it changes the type of data that can be collected for market survey purposes. Looking forward, real estate negotiations certified through Blockchain protocols would reduce the risk associated with incomplete and incorrect information and increase the quality of data used by investors and real estate users (Deloitte, 2017).

3.4 Conclusion

Technology is now a necessary minimum standard for property management, and in recent years the weight of technology applications has grown even in smaller and less valuable properties. The goals pursued through the use of protection solutions are to minimize the risks involved in various real estate investments and to make online solutions such tools available even to investors with limited assets for whom the development of proprietary solutions would not make economic sense. Proptech companies have been the primary tool for the widespread use of technology within the real estate industry. They have speeded up the innovation process that would otherwise have taken traditional operators several years.

The technology is being applied to manage both real estate development and redevelopment interventions and operations that involve putting the property to income and allow for managing and reducing the risk associated with the investment made. The proptech solutions available on the market can be for recurring operations that must be carried out throughout the entire view of the project, operations that require the collection and processing of a significant amount of data, or extraordinary processes to be carried out on a one-off basis during the investment.

References

Barkham, R. (2002). Market research for office real estate. In S. Guy & J. Henneberry (Eds.), *Development and developers: Perspectives on property*. Blackwell Publishing.

Battisti, E., Riad Shams, S. M., Sakka, G., & Miglietta, N. (2020). Big data and risk management in business processes: Implications for corporate real estate. *Business Process Management Journal, 26*(5), 1141–1155.

Bröchner, J., Haugen, T., & Lindkvist, C. (2019). Shaping tomorrow's facilities management. *Facilities, 37*(7/8), 366–380.

Cerasoli, M., & Mattarocci, G. (2021). La rendita come strumento di rilancio del riuso intelligente (e contro l'insostenibile cultura del nuovo). *Valori e Valutazioni, 27*, 1–10.

Crockett, J. (1982). Competition and efficiency in transacting: The case of residential real estate brokerage. *AREUEA Journal, 10*(2), 209–227.

D'Arcy, E., & Keogh, G. (2002). The market context of property development activities. In S. Guy & J. Henneberry (Eds.), *Development and developers: Perspectives on property*. Blackwell Publishing.

DeLisle, J. R., Never, B., & Grissom, T. V. (2020). The big data regime shift in real estate. *Journal of Property Investment & Finance, 38*(4), 363–395.

Deloitte. (2017). *Blockchain in commercial real estate: The future is here.* Accessed January 30, 2021, from https://www2.deloitte.com/.

Fields D. (2022) Automated landlord: Digital technologies and post-crisis financial accumulation. *Environment and Planning: A Economy and Space, 54*(1), 160–181.

Flanagan, R., & Norman, G. (2003). *Risk management and construction.* Blackwell Publishing.

Gabriel, S. A., & Nothaft, F. E. (1988). Rental housing markets and the natural vacancy rate. *AREUEA Journal, 16*(4), 419–429.

Gabriel, S. A., & Nothaft, F. E. (2001). Rental housing markets, the incidence and duration of vacancy and the natural vacancy rate. *Journal of Urban Economics, 49*(1), 121–149.

Gehner E. (2008). *Knowingly taking risk Investment decision making in real estate development.* Eburon Academic Publishers, Delft.

Guttentag, D. (2019). Progress on Airbnb: A literature review. *Journal of Hospitality and Tourism Technology, 10*(4), 814–844.

Haurin, D. (1988). The duration of marketing time or residential housing. *AREUEA Journal, 16*(4), 396–410.

Hess, R., & Liang, H. (2003). Decomposing the recent office market vacancy spike. *Real Estate Finance, 19*(6), 12–19.

Hettenhouse, G. W., & Dee, J. J. (1976). A component analysis of rates of return in real estate investment. *AREUEA Journal, 4*(1), 7–21.

Huffman, F. E. (2002). Corporate real estate risk management and assessment. *Journal of Corporate Real Estate, 5*(1), 31–41.

JLL. (2021). *The impact of COVID-19 on flexible space. What the future holds in a fast-paced world affected by the pandemic.* Accessed January 30, 2021, from https://www.us.jll.com/.

Karamitsos, I., Papadaki, M., & Al Barghuthi, N. B. (2018). Design of the blockchain smart contract: A use case for real estate. *Journal of Information Security, 9*, 177–190.

Kejriwal, S., & Mahajan, S. (2016). *Smart buildings: How IoT Technology aims to add value for real estate companies. The Internet of Things in the CRE industry.* Accessed January 30, 2021, from www2.deloitte.com.

Kim, T. (2019). Venture capital, startups and commercial real estate: Innovation potential in a bespoke industry. *Corporate Real Estate Journal, 8*(3), 204–209.

Lai, H., Deng, X., & Chang, T. Y. (2019). BIM-based platform for collaborative building design and project management. *Journal of Computing in Civil Engineering, 33*(3), 1–15.

Lecomte, P. (2020). iSpace: Principles for a phenomenology of space user in smart real estate. *Journal of Property Investment & Finance, 38*(4), 271–290.

Li, L., & Chau, K. W. (2019). What motivates a developer to sell before completion? *Journal of Real Estate Finance and Economics, 59*(1), 209–232.

Ling, D. (1994). The price of owner occupied housing services 1973-1989. In J. De Lisle & J. S. Aadu (Eds.), *Real estate research issues* (Vol. 1, pp. 425–462). Kluwer Academic.

Lecomte, P. (2019). What is smart? A real estate introduction to cities and buildings in the digital era. *Journal of General Management, 44*(3), 128–137.

Maalsee, S., & Dowling, R. (2020). Covid 19 and the accelerating smart home. *Big Data & Society, 7*(2), 1–5.

McAfee, A., & Brynjolfsson, E. (2012). Big data: The management revolution. *Harvard Business Review, 10*, 1–9.

Mcdonald, J. F. (2000). Rent, vacancy and equilibrium in real estate markets. *Journal of Real Estate Practice and Education, 3*(1), 55–69.

McKinsey. (2018). *Getting ahead of the market: How big data is transforming real estate.* Accessed January 30, 2021, from https://www.mckinsey.com/.

Mueller, G. R. (1999). Real estate rental growth rates at different points in the physical market cycle. *Journal of Real Estate Research, 18*(1), 131–150.

Plattner, R. H. (1988). *Real estate investment. Analysis and management.* Merril Publish.

Roulac, S. (2019). The Industrial Revolution remembers. *Journal of Property Investment and Finance, 37*(4), 380–397.

Short, P., Minnery, J., Mead, E., Adkins, B., Peake, A., Fredrick, D., & O'Flaherty, M. (2003). *Tenancy databases: Risk minimization and outcomes.* Australian Housing and Urban Research Institute research paper.

Springer, T. M., & Waller, N. G. (1996). Maintenance of residential rental property: An empirical analysis. *Journal of Real Estate Research, 12*(1), 89–99.

Starr, C. W., Saginor, J., & Worzala, E. (2020). The rise of PropTech: Emerging industrial technologies and their impact on real estate. *Journal of Property Investment & Finance, 39*(2), 157–169.

Sullivan, C., & Fisher, R. M. (1988). Consumer credit delinquency: Characteristics of consumers who fall behind. *Journal of Retail Banking, 10*, 53–64.

Wheaton, W. C., & Torto, R. G. (1998). Vacancy rates and the future of office rents. *AREUEA Journal, 16*(4), 430–436.

Wilkinson, S. J., & Jupp, J. R. (2016). Exploring the value of BIM for corporate real estate. *Journal of Corporate Real Estate, 18*(4), 254–269.

Wincott, R. (1997). *Vacancy rate and reasonableness* (pp. 361–370). *Appraisal Journal.*

Worzala, E., Souza, L. A., Koroleva, O., Martin, C., Becker, A., & Derrick, N. (2021). The technological impact on real estate investing: Robots vs humans: New applications for organisational and portfolio strategies. *Journal of Property Investment & Finance, 39*(2), 170–177.

CHAPTER 4

Real Estate Negotiation Tools

Abstract Real estate transactions suffer from a lack of transparency and liquidity, making the investment riskier from the investors' point of view. Technology has radically improved the quality of the service that companies may provide for supporting real estate trades and reduced the time on the market of real estate assets.

The chapter discusses the real estate transaction risk and the main solution offered by protech companies for reducing the time spent in the initial screening, increasing the quality of the value forecast, matching the need of supply and demand, and for certifying the quality of the information available.

Keywords Transaction risk • Screening • Valuation • Negotiation • Due diligence • Time on the market

4.1 INTRODUCTION

Real estate investment is, by definition, illiquid. The critical issues for investors are to select the best investment opportunity and identify the optimal holding period based on the transaction cost and the risk related to the asset value volatility (Brueggeman et al., 1981). The degree of liquidity for each real estate asset is unique and related to the transaction profile, the community characteristics, the neighboring services, and the market trend of the day on the market (Zu et al., 2016).

The real estate market is an information-intensive and information-driven industry. Negotiation could be affected by the possibility of having more and better information for adequately evaluating the risk exposure (Kumar, 2014). The choice of investing in real estate is typically affected by the quality of data available. Especially for some market and real estate assets, the availability of high-quality information is the pre-condition for any possible negotiation.

Negotiation in the real estate market involves different companies/ individuals that help match the buyer's needs with the supply of real estate units in the market (Stevens & Zhu, 2010). Services are related to the advisory service for identifying the investment opportunity, consultancy for setting the correct price or rent for the asset, brokerage activities for promoting the building or the real estate unit in the market, and due diligence activities necessary for completing the transaction.

This chapter describes the real estate transaction risk, underlines the role of information asymmetry in the real estate market (Sect. 4.2), and analyzes IT and proptech solutions for supporting the liquidity and the efficiency of the real estate market (Sect. 4.3).

4.2   Real Estate Transaction Risk

Real estate investment is a durable asset characterized by a low level of information transparency that may need to be managed to balance the needs of the two counterparties and avoid one party taking undue advantage of the situation of information asymmetry. Thus, real estate negotiations are highly exposed to the risks associated with information asymmetry, which can lead to talks between actors with a significant information gap, as assumed in the "market of lemons" model (Akerlof, 1970).

Real estate markets are quite different in terms of regulation applied and transparency, even in the developed market (JLL, 2020, 2022) (Table 4.1).

In the last years, for almost all the markets, the attention given to transparency issues has grown, and the quality of the information provided for all the stages of the negotiation process has increased. Perfectly efficient markets are minimal, and only the most relevant market worldwide (like the UK) could ensure the best transparency standards.

In the case of negotiations between real estate developers and buyers, project-based purchasing is often used to facilitate the completion of the project and reduce the cost of raising capital for the company during the

Table 4.1 Information transparency in EU 28 real estate markets

Country	2018	2020	2022
Austria	2.23	2.32	n.a.
Belgium	2.08	1.99	1.10
Bulgaria	3.11	2.87	1.92
Czech Republic	2.26	2.41	1.25
Cyprus	n.a.	n.a.	n.a.
Croatia	3.01	3.00	1.63
Denmark	2.11	2.10	1.00
Estonia	n.a.	n.a.	n.a.
Finland	1.95	1.98	1.27
France	1.44	1.44	1.00
Germany	1.88	1.93	1.30
Greece	2.94	2.86	2.13
Hungary	2.44	2.44	1.53
Ireland	1.93	1.83	1.00
Italy	2.12	2.08	1.33
Latvia	n.a.	n.a	n.a.
Lithuania	n.a.	n.a	n.a.
Luxembourg	2.65	2.59	1.45
Malta	n.a.	n.a.	2.78
Netherlands	1.51	1.67	1.15
Poland	2.15	2.24	1.43
Portugal	2.30	2.42	1.23
Romania	2.49	2.71	1.48
Slovakia	2.40	2.44	1.53
Slovenia	3.06	3.32	1.63
Spain	2.14	2.16	1.17
Sweden	1.93	1.89	1.30
United Kingdom	1.24	1.31	1.00

Notes: The score varies from 1 to 5, and higher values of the index identify countries with lower transparency

Source: JLL (2020, 2022) data processed by the authors

life of the construction site. From the buyer's point of view, this solution makes it possible to reduce the overall price paid by offering a pre-payment of a percentage of the amount due and by entering into the contract early as the owner of a building under construction.

The risks associated with project-based purchase contracts are related not only to the dynamics of real estate prices after the contract is signed but also to the risks associated with the final asset's quality and the delivery timing to the user (Ong, 1999).

The phase of sale or lease by a landlord to a buyer or tenant always sees an information gap to the disadvantage of the buyer or tenant, who may have access to the same information set as the seller and is exposed to the risk of overpricing the property. The solutions adopted in different countries apply constraints to sellers regarding the minimum data set to be made available in the real estate transaction. Still, the information asymmetry problem often cannot be remedied by simple transparency constraints on the traded property. There are usually costs associated with the increased transparency required (Chau & Choi, 2011). The cost associated with collecting information necessary for compliance with disclosure requirements to be transmitted to the market cannot only be a significant burden for the seller. Still, it can also, in some cases, represent a service that is not perfectly usable by the buyer/lessor, given that excessive detail in the transmitted disclosure may disincentivize the end user to pay attention to the inside product document (Ma et al., 2018).

The level of information asymmetry is also related to the specific characteristics of the commodity being traded, which may result in greater or lesser interest of the parties to invest resources to reduce the information asymmetry before proceeding with the trade. More complex and significant transactions, therefore, see agents and appraisers making fair judgments about the sale price and limiting the extra-profit opportunities that the seller/lessee can obtain by using their informational advantage (Ong & Brown, 2001). The effectiveness of the agency mechanism is related to the amount of commission that the individual agent can earn and consequently to that professional's interest in contributing to the successful outcome and success of the transaction (Anglin & Arnott, 1991).

The relevance of information asymmetry is related to the inherent characteristics of the market in which the property is traded, given that the asset has, by definition, unique and distinctive qualities that can be more fairly valued if the investor knows the dynamics of area prices for similar properties. Regardless of the type of asset, residential or commercial, the level of transparency increases as market liquidity increases because the availability of a large dataset on prices and rents related to transactions in the area for similar properties allows for more reliable estimates of the value of the property (Garmaise & Moskowitz, 2004). For the same property, buyers who have already purchased or leased properties in the area suffer from a smaller information gap vis-à-vis the landlord, and this profile may put them in a position to pay lower prices or rents per square meter and consequently increase their affordability to carry out the transaction (Kurlat & Stroebel, 2015).

The real estate purchase process is divided into four stages before reaching the completion of the transaction that allows the two parties to gather all the information necessary for the successful completion of the trade and involve the different actors who will be involved in the transaction (Tita, 2012) (Fig. 4.1).

The first step in the sales process involves the submission of a letter of intent, which is a necessary first step before entering into a contract specifying the terms of the agreement, which is currently being negotiated by the parties and is not a binding contract for the parties.

The irrevocable purchase proposal is the first binding document entered by the parties in which the buyer declares his interest in purchasing the property by setting its price and defining the time horizon of validity of the proposal, after which the seller will no longer have the right to accept the bid. The proposal is usually submitted together with a security deposit that will be used to pay the penalty if the buyer decides or is unable to enter into the final purchase and sale agreement, and which is the parameter against which the sentence is to be paid if the seller counterparty decides not to succeed in the contract is determined. The contract may provide for termination conditions upon the occurrence of which the obligation of the parties to perform the agreement ceases, and neither party is obligated to pay the penalties stipulated in the contract.

The preliminary (or Pro-forma) contract may be drafted to define in detail the obligations of the parties and give the buyer, if necessary, all the elements for applying for financing connected with the purchase and the seller time to gather, if not yet available, the documents required for completing the transaction. In countries such as Italy, where there is a provision for this, the deed can also be registered to give maximum legal protection to the parties involved in the transaction.

The negotiation is concluded with the signing of the sale and purchase agreement, which transfers the property outright to the new owner against

Fig. 4.1 Contracts for real estate negotiation. Source: Authors' elaboration

payment of the amount agreed upon in the contract and can be carried out on the individual real estate unit or a group of properties. In countries such as Italy, where it is provided, the deed must be registered by a notarial deed.

The stipulation of a lease of a property is more flexible and provides for a simple agreement between the parties on the terms of the contract. In some markets, there may not even be an obligation to stipulate in writing in the case of real estate for residential use. The agreement must clearly state the property and its cadastral data, the contractual conditions applied, and the contract expiration dates with different deadlines depending on the type of contract entered into and the taxation regime to which one wishes to have access. The agreement provides for the tenant to pay a deposit at the time of stipulation that will be used to indemnify the landlord in case of any damage done to the property and minimum pre-notice constraints that must be met to close the contract.

4.3   Transaction Support Tools

Buying or leasing a property can be divided according to the counterparties involved and the main activities that will characterize the process. The standard classification distinguishes (Fig. 4.2):

The following subsections will analyze the role of proptech solutions in each stage of the negotiation process. They will provide some examples of opportunities offered by technology in real estate truncation management.

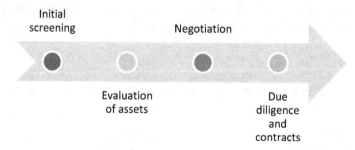

Fig. 4.2   Stage of the negotiation process. Source: Authors' elaboration

4.3.1   Initial Screening

The search for properties to buy or rent is carried out by finding the property most consistent with the user's availability and needs. An initial assessment is conducted through online platforms that gather information on opportunities in a particular area. The media may be agency-owned or, more frequently, storefronts through which data on different properties are made available regardless of an agent's presence and company. The features most requested by platform users are the number of listings posted, the effectiveness of the selection filter, the controls on the posted listings, the amount of context information collected for each sale and rental listing, and the ability to use the tool to make direct comparisons between available opportunities (Betzeki, 2020).

The business model of the real estate platforms could be classified as follows (Cherif & Grant, 2014):

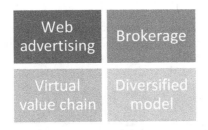

Web advertising is the simpler business model adopted by platforms that offer a solution to landlords for promoting their real estate assets without charging them a fee. The source of income is related to the opportunity to sell promotion pages to companies for other types of goods and services. The main advantage of IT technology is the profiling tools that allow customizing the advertising based on the user's preferences.

The brokerage solution offers platforms that allow searching for a real estate investment opportunity by providing sufficient information for a pre-screening among all the available assets. The company managing the web portal usually requests a fee for the service provided from both the buyer/tenant and the seller/landlord proportional to the value of the real estate asset.

The virtual value chain allows obtaining profit by using and processing information by creating products and services in the form of digital information delivered through information-based channels.

The diversified model attains to companies that are members of diversified groups that are offering different types of goods and services, and that may use the platform also for cross-selling activities in the interest of the group. This solution has pros and cons but may be implemented only if the real estate players are affiliated with a group offering goods and services that may interest their real estate customers.

Big data and applications available in the cloud make it possible to reduce the time required to analyze available investment opportunities through automated investment profiling algorithms that, once the target rate of return on investment is defined, allow for the selection of properties on the market in an area that may be consistent with stated investment objectives (Miles et al., 2019).

4.3.2   Evaluation of Assets

The analysis of investment opportunities relies on the study of comparables in the same area to measure the value per square meter for rent or sale. Data quality and reliability are a prerequisite for making this assessment. The choice among comparable assets has to consider:

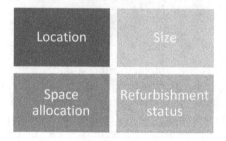

The location is one of the main drivers of the real estate value, and the analysis has not to be limited only to the city but also to the area in the town may matter especially if the quality of the (public or private) services provided is different in each district of the city.

The size of the asset matters because the real estate market (for both ownership and rent) offers significant discounts for large ticket transactions due to the lower number of buyers or tenants potentially interested in investing in the building due to the higher minimum capital required.

The allocation of spaces modifies the usage opportunities for the tenant or the buyer; typically, more flexible solutions are more requested by the market and more expensive. Buildings characterized by not flexible layout may suffer from changing users' needs, making some assets developed with old construction standards less appealing to the market.

The year of construction and the time from the last major refurbishment affect the market demand for the real estate asset because older and poorly maintained real estate assets are generally offered at a discount. The importance of the time of construction/refurbishment has been growing in the last year due to the innovation in the technology typically used in the buildings.

Comparison of market data (prices and rents at first request) with the value of registered contracts in an area has revealed significant misalignments that make cadastral data out of date and of little use in setting the price or rent to be demanded in the market and has therefore created a need to develop applications that can work on big data and provide timely, real-time valuations for properties in the vicinity (Boeing et al., forthcoming).

Platforms can also offer the ability to create a network that includes buyer/lessee and seller/landlord, and expert appraisers who can support the parties in setting a fair price. The platform, in this case, offers a brokerage service by selecting a pool of accredited appraisers in the forum and to whom the application requests that platform users have sent are submitted. The added value of the service is related to the ability to identify qualified experts and the possibility, given a large number of users, to offer the service at competitive costs (Fields & Rogers, 2021).

ICT can be a tool to standardize property valuation processes using computer-aided valuation systems (CAVs) that, especially in less developed markets, in terms of training and average skills of valuers, can radically change the approach to valuation (Uwaifiokun A., 2019). The valuation mechanism that CAV models use involves collecting data on transactions in the market for properties of the same type and extrapolating the property's value based on an algorithm based on a hedonic model (Kok et al., 2017).

4.3.3   Negotiation

Platforms to facilitate contact between seller/landlord and buyer/tenant are now a standard for asset management, even though the product has evolved dramatically in recent years to meet the parties' needs. The main advantage associated with the online channel compared to traditional channels with ads in real estate or the daily press is related to the detail of information surveyed, the number of ads considered, and the ability to filter data according to the specific needs of the individual client (Boeing et al., 2021)

The most innovative platforms make it possible to make available to potential tenants or buyers not only floor plans and photos of the real estate unit but also 3-D videos that reduce the time spent by likely interested parties for the first inspection and speed up the sale or lease process (Kummerow & Chan, 2005). More advanced 3D solutions include creating avatars with which the potential client can interact with an agent, thus making the virtual visit to the property even more effective (Hagl & Duane, 2020).

The success of a real estate negotiation is also linked to the characteristics and experience of the agent/broker following the transaction, their ability to identify clients' needs (sellers and buyers) and mediate the parties' needs (Crockett, 1982). The most innovative solutions made available on Internet channels make it possible to evaluate the broker chosen to follow the transaction (seller-side or buyer-side) by systematically collecting information about past transactions and the satisfaction level of the parties involved.

In recent years, real estate investors have often experienced liquidity problems that have necessitated the sale of properties. In a scarcely liquid market, the value of the occupied property can be, especially for the low residential segment. Innovative tools to address this need include online marketplaces in which property characteristics and profitability based on existing leases are promoted to allow financing partners to be found for an investment in a leased property (Fields, 2022). In the case of commercial real estate, the platform also offers data on the tenant that allows for the assessment of the counterparty's reliability, the sustainability of the rent in the medium to long term, and the characteristics and clauses applied to the lease (Xiaofang et al., 2013).

The supply of space for rent and sale has evolved in recent years with the growth of solutions related to the concept of the sharing economy that makes it possible to maximize the number of users of the space and, consequently, reduce the service cost offered. In the rental market, products have been developed that allow to view and book the use of facilities for limited times by entering into contracts that will enable using a facility for a maximum number of hours within a month or the time horizon chosen by the tenant. This solution has been particularly effective for commercial properties such as offices (co-working spaces) and spaces within stores or shopping centers (temporary exhibitions) (Mattarocci & Roberti, 2019). In the property market, shared property purchase solutions (timeshare) are a well-established solution for the residential market and protect solutions that have not changed the business model but have made it possible to offer services related to timeshare (maintenance, property cleaning, etc...) and have facilitated the mechanism of exchanging the right of use between different owners to make the use of the service more attractive. The potential of the network has also made it possible to develop methods of alternative use of owned residential properties by facilitating the development of entrepreneurial ventures in the hotel sector in a broad sense by allowing at a reduced cost to use part of one's home for Bed & Breakfast activity (Sainz, 2020).

4.3.4 Due Diligence and Contracts

Currently, available technology allows for the construction of transaction settlement models based on Blockchain technology to reduce some risks characterizing the sale or lease of real estate. The simple cryptographic signature is an effective solution for signing online contracts but is still highly exposed to the risk of forgery. In contrast, the protocol solution further reduces the risk of unauthorized transactions by the rightful owners and allows for certification of the quality of contracts and professional valuations (FIBREE, 2019). To date, experience in the real estate sector is less than in other sectors of the economy, but there are ample growth opportunities shortly.

Blockchain technology applied to real estate negotiations makes it possible to speed up the sale and lease process by transforming the documents and certificates linked to the individual property into a single encrypted code that can be analyzed and decrypted by everyone in the network (FIBREE, 2019). Pilot studies have been carried out on the possibility of using the Blockchain tool for the online land register to make the service fully digital, make much of the information available and verifiable on the network, and leave only the data strictly covered by privacy privileged access.

Evidence of the tool's effectiveness has demonstrated the feasibility of the intervention and the potential economic benefits associated with its implementation while highlighting only a few critical, potentially solvable issues related to the risks of identity theft and, more generally, cybersecurity (Salmeling & Fransson, 2017). The advantages for the real estate sector are mainly related to the commercial industry in which several counterparties involved in the property management (landlord, tenant, building manager, facility manager, lenders, appraisers) are involved. The adoption of standardized Blockchain-type protocols could also overcome any problems related to information exchanges between the information systems of the different parties (Veuger, 2020). The entire process managed through Blockchain facilitates the due diligence of the property, both fiscal and urban planning points, by abating the time required to collect the necessary data (Fig. 4.3).

The operation mechanism of transactions based on Blockchain-type technology involves registering contracts for purchasing and leasing the property (1) and all warranties related to trading. The investments made by the seller/landlord for the management of the property (4) and the administration of services (5), and the related certifications/attestations issued are directly recorded through the Blockchain. If the land register is sufficiently automated, the property characteristics and urban planning data are transferred from the land registry directly to the Blockchain protocol, and there is almost no risk of losing some relevant information about the ownership of the building (2). If the investment is not realized by cash, financing solution and mortgages are recorded using the same technology, and everyone can quickly check (3). The due diligence process is simplified because all documentation of the individual property is accessible from the Blockchain (6).

The cost associated with moving from the current registration system to one based on the Blockchain protocol can be justified according to the increased ability to track all transactions related to the individual property and, consequently, the increased flows associated with taxation on the property and related activities (Proskurovska & Dorry, 2018).

Fig. 4.3 Process managed through Blockchain. Source: Authors' elaboration

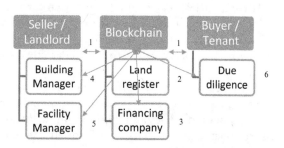

The most significant opportunities in the short term related to the use of Blockchain-type protocol are related to international demand for investment in a country's real estate sector. Recent analyses of major European markets have shown substantial differences in the detail of pre-contract and contract information, land registry procedures, financing opportunities, and practices applied by agents in negotiations (Sparkes et al., 2017). The standardization and transparency of the talks carried out with the new technology could strongly incentivize investment by foreign nationals who are currently disincentivized from investing in Italy, given the high complexity and riskiness associated with the different stages of real estate investment (Nasarre-Aznar, 2018).

4.4 Conclusion

A lack of efficiency characterizes real estate and limited liquidity that does not allow to assume the price and the rent are always at their fair price, and there are no market frictions. Real estate transactions involve parties other than the buyer/tenant and the seller/landlord, and information technology may minimize transaction costs.

Proptech companies may construct their business model focusing on the services requested to identify the investment opportunities available, for the definition of the price/rent of the asset, for the title of the prospective tenant or buyer, and/or the due diligence service. Technology innovation offers opportunities for developing new services and exciting products for owners and users of real estate assets. The main advantage offered is the opportunity to have more information about the risk assumed and reduce the time necessary for completing the negotiation.

In the initial screening process, the leading requested service is a more detailed and complete set of data for each property, reducing the number of on-site visits necessary for the investment choice. In the evaluation stage, the asset's pricing or the acceptable rent level must be identified by mixing different data sources, and AI may help standardize the process. The negotiation stage may benefit from technology because the higher the quality and amount of data immediately available for the owner, the higher the possibility of customizing the contract based on the buyer's specific needs, so the higher the probability of success in the negotiation. In the due diligence stage nowadays, the technology is the standard requested by the market for creating data rooms and has multiple counterparties that provide services to the building and the users.

References

Akerlof, G. A. (1970). The market for "lemons": Quality uncertainty and the market mechanism. *Quarterly Journal of Economics, 84*(3), 488–500.

Anglin, P. M., & Arnott, R. (1991). Residential real estate brokerage as a principal-agent problem. *Journal of Real Estate Finance and Economics, 4*(1), 99–125.

Betzeki, C. (2020). *PropTech: Exploring the prerequisites to advance the digital innovation of real estate listings.* Retrieved January 30, 2021, from https://www.diva-portal.org/.

Boeing, G., Wegmann, J., & Jiao, J. (forthcoming). Rental housing spot markets: How online information exchanges can supplement transacted-rents data. *Journal of Planning Education and Research,* 1–13.

Boeing, G., Besbris, M., Schacter, A., & Kuk, J. (2021). housing search in the age of big data: Smarter cities or the same old blind spots? *Housing Policy Debate, 31*(1), 112–126.

Brueggeman, W., Fisher, J., & Stern, J. (1981). Federal income taxes, inflation and holding periods for income-producing properties. *AREUEA Journal, 9*(2), 148–164.

Cherif, E., & Grant, D. (2014). Analysis of e-business models in real estate. *Electronic Commerce Research, 14*(1), 25–50.

Chau, K. W., & Choy, L. H. T. (2011). Let the buyer or seller beware: Measuring lemons in the housing market under different doctrines of law governing transactions and information. *Journal of Law and Economics, 54*(4), S347–SS65.

Crockett, J. H. (1982). Competition and efficiency in transacting: The case of residential real estate brokerage. *Real Estate Economics, 10*(2), 209–227.

FIBREE. (2019). *FIBREE industry report blockchain real estate 2019.* Accessed September 01, 2022 from https://fibree.org/.

Fields D. (2022) Automated landlord: Digital technologies and post-crisis financial accumulation. *Environment and Planning: A Economy and Space, 54*(1), 160–181.

Fields, D., & Rogers, D. (2021). Towards a critical housing studies research agenda on platform real estate. *Housing, Theory and Society, 38*(1), 72–84.

Garmaise, M. J., & Moskowitz, T. J. (2004). Confronting information asymmetries: Evidence from real estate markets. *Review of Financial Studies, 17*(2), 405–437.

Hagl, R., & Duante, A. (2020). Applying business model innovation to real estate distribution by employing virtual reality and artificial intelligence a report from praxis. In *6th International AR & VR Conference proceedings.*

JLL. (2020). *Global Real Estate Transparency Index 2020.* Retrieved January 30, 2021, from www.jll.it.

JLL. (2022). *Global Real Estate Transparency Index 2022.* Retrieved January 30, 2021, from www.jll.it.

Kok, N., Koponen, E. L., & Martínez-Barbosa, C. A. (2017). Big data in real estate? From manual appraisal to automated valuation. *Journal of Portfolio Management, 43*(6), 202–211.

Kumar, B. (2014). Impact of digital marketing and e-commerce on the real estate industry. *International Journal of Research in Business Management, 2*(7), 17–22.

Kurlat, P., & Stroebel, J. (2015). Testing for information asymmetries in real estate markets. *Review of Financial Studies, 28*(8), 2429–2461.

Kummerow, M., & Chan, L. J. (2005). Information and communication technology in the real estate industry: Productivity, industry structure, and market efficiency. *Telecommunication Policy, 29*(2–3), 173–190.

Ma, S. Y. T., Chan, E. H. W., & Choy, L. H. T. (2018). Evolving institutions to tackle asymmetrical information problems in the housing market: A case study on 'shrinkage' of flat sizes in Hong Kong. *Habitat International, 75*(1), 154–160.

Mattarocci, G., & Roberti, S. (2019). Proptech, le nuove strade del mercato immobiliare. *Bancaria, 75*(10), 83–91.

Mills, J., Molloy, R., & Zarutskie, R. (2019). Large-scale buy-to-rent investors in the single-family housing market: The emergence of a new asset class. *Real Estate Economics, 47*(2), 399–430.

Nasarre-Aznar, S. (2018). Collaborative housing and blockchain. *Administration, 66*(2), 59–82.

Ong, S. E. (1999). Caveat emptor: Adverse selection in buying properties under construction. *Property Management, 17*(1), 49–64.

Ong, S. E., & Brown, G. (2001). Information issue in real estate. *Pacific Rim Property Research Journal, 7*(1), 61–72.

Proskurovska, A., & Dorry, S. (2018). *Is a Blockchain-based conveyance system the next step in the financialization of housing? The case of Sweden.* LISER Working Paper Series 2018-17.

Salmeling, M., & Fransson, C. (2017). *The land registry in the blockchain-testbed. A development project with Lantmäteriet, Landshypotek Bank, SBAB, Telia Company, ChromaWay, and Kairos Future.* Retrieved January 30, 2021, from www.chromaway.com/.

Saiz, A. (2020). Bricks, mortar, and proptech: The economics of IT in brokerage, space utilization, and commercial real estate finance. *Journal of Property Investment & Finance, 38*(4), 327–347.

Sparkes, P., Bulut, D., Habdas, M., Jordan, M., Moreno, H. S., Nasarre-Aznar, S., Ralli, T., & Strutz, M. (2017). *What everyone got wrong about Fiverr's 'Doer' campaign.* Retrieved January 30, 2021, from http://www.thedrum.com.

Stevens, D. P., & Zhu, Z. (2010). An approach to service innovation in real estate through information technology. *International Journal of Services and Standards, 6*(1), 79–84.

Tita, G. (2012). I contratti dell'operazione di compravendita immobilaire. In C. Cacciamani (Ed.), *Real Estate. Economia, diritto, marketing e finanza immobiliare*. EGEA.

Uwaifiokun, A. V. (2019). The PropTech revolution: The imperatives for Nigeria's estate surveying and valuation professionals to catch up or get left behind. *Journal of African Real Estate Research, 4*(2), 56–75.

Veuger, J. (2020). Dutch blockchain, real estate, and land registration. *Journal of Property, Planning and Environmental Law, 12*(2), 93–108.

Xiaofang, Y., Ji-Hyun, L., Sun-Joong, K., & Yoon-Hyun, K. (2013). Towards a user-oriented recommendation system for real estate websites. *Information Systems, 38*(2), 231–243.

Zhu, H., Xiong, H., Tang, F., Liu, Q., Ge, Y., Chen, E., & Fu, Y. (2016). *Days on market: Measuring liquidity in real estate markets*. Proceedings of the 22nd ACM SIGKDD International Conference on Knowledge Discovery and Data Mining (KDD '16), Association for Computing Machinery, New York, NY.

CHAPTER 5

Financing Instruments: Focus on P2P Lending and Crowdfunding

Abstract Fintech companies represent the new frontier of financial intermediation worldwide. The real estate market is one of the more attractive industries in which the new players can compete with the traditional financial institutions.

This chapter considers both equity and debt crowdfunding. It points out the main differences concerning traditional financial solutions showing both the opportunities and the risks related to the new approach. The discussion presented will also consider the issues related to regulation and the impact of the difference in the regulatory framework on the development of the market.

Keywords Peer-to-Peer • Debt crowdfunding • Equity crowdfunding • Alternative financing

5.1 Introduction

Following the recent revolution given by Fintech in financial markets (Arner et al., 2015), the phenomenon of Proptech has become a significant element of interest in the context of Financial Technology applied to the real estate sector.

Proptech is not an entirely recent phenomenon and can be defined as the use of new digital products within the real estate sector (Baum, 2017):

Definition "software-based platforms that optimize the purchase and sale of real estates, such as classic real estate properties and/or shares of funds or shares invested in assets included in real estate." (Feth & Gruneberg, 2018)

These platforms are known by the acronym REC (Real Estate Crowdfunding).

Real estate crowdfunding is a way to raise funds for real estate investments, thanks to a pool of lenders who, with a small amount of money, participate in the success of a project. Simply put, it is a form of capital raising that allows small real estate investors to finance large projects. It is also referred to as peer-to-peer lending.

The fundraising process is conducted through an online crowdfunding platform in which one party (the borrower) has the objective of obtaining the necessary resources to start or improve a real estate project; another party (the investor/lender) wants to invest capital in exchange for high returns.

Although the real estate sector tends to be a "conservative sector" (which explains the slow use of digital products in this field), there is no doubt that the introduction of digital platforms is a way to ensure liquidity and greater efficiency in this market.

Historically, it is difficult to determine when crowdfunding began (Belezas, 2017). Still, the very first initiatives in this sector can be traced back to 2002, when the Blender Foundation, a non-profit company to cope with the financial difficulties caused by the sales reduction associated with the dot.com crisis (Moris & Pervaiz, 2008), launched a crowdfunding campaign to financially support its project: a widely used three-dimensional animation software developed by a Dutch company called Not a Number (Belleflamme et al., 2013). This campaign reached the necessary amount of money (€100,000) in just seven weeks.

Unlike regular crowdfunding, they were creating the first REC platform that is newer and easier to determine. Fundraise, founded in 2010 and focused on the American market, was the first platform in the world to invest in the real estate sector.

As with generic crowdfunding, the REC has blossomed after a period of crisis. It has been seen as an essential alternative to traditional financing channels since the subprime mortgage crisis in 2008 (Gilliland, 2017) when banks were more reluctant to provide financing. Since then, there has been an increase in similar platforms worldwide: CrowdStreet, Groundfloor, and RealCrowd are just a few examples of REC platforms developed immediately after Fundraise. Through some of these platforms, each person can invest in different real estate projects with only 10 dollars.

In this chapter, we will analyze how crowdfunding and P2P lending work in general terms, then go down precisely to the two alternatives that can be used for financing in real estate: debt crowdfunding and equity crowdfunding.

5.2   The Classification of P2P Lending in Crowdfunding

The concept of crowdfunding is part of the broader topic of crowdsourcing, a term used for the first time in 2006 by Jeff Howe and Mark Robinson in an American high-tech magazine, Wired Magazine.

In 2008, Kleemann proposed the first definition, arguing that crowdsourcing occurs when a company outsources specific tasks for manufacturing or selling its products. This outsourcing is done to the public (i.e., the "crowd") in the form of an open call on the Internet. This call intends to encourage people to voluntarily contribute to the company's production process to contribute to the company's production process voluntarily.

This definition seems to have been a good starting point for Belleflamme, Lambert, and Schwienbacher, who in 2010 defined crowdfunding as:

Definition "something that involves an open call, essentially through the internet, to provide financial resources to a company through donation and investment."

The European Crowdfunding Network 2012 defines it as the commitment of many individuals to put their financial resources on a network to support activities started by other people or organizations. Financing for individual projects and businesses usually takes place through small contributions from many subjects, allowing entrepreneurs to raise capital through their social networks.

Instead, Lehner and Harrer (2019) argue that crowdfunding relies on the aggregate financial power of many non-institutionalized individuals who engage in a particular form of entrepreneurial financing (Fig. 5.1).

TRADITIONAL LENDING   CROWDFUNDING

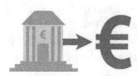   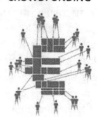

Large ticked loans offered from   Small loans offered from many
     one or few lenders   lenders

Fig. 5.1 Operation of traditional financing vs. Crowdfunding. Source: European Commission, 2015, "Crowdfunding: what it is"

Crowdfunding can also be considered as a two-sided market, in which, within a network, there are two distinct groups of users: on the one hand, the investors who contribute to the fundraising, and on the other hand, subjects (companies or consumers) looking for funds (Bouncken et al., 2015).

It is, therefore, possible to see how at least three distinctive elements fall into every definition of crowdfunding (Pais et al., 2018): fundraising, the crowd, and the use of the Internet.

There are three different types of actors involved (Tomczak & Brem, 2013):

- Intermediaries: who deal with providing standardized processes for each investor or fund applicant. Intermediaries are distinguished according to their focus: there are specific platforms for creative projects, corporate projects, or fundraising projects in the narrower sense (Zvilichovsky et al., 2015);
- Individuals: in search of loans (borrowers) who, thanks to crowdfunding, can obtain the financial resources they need. Since crowdfunding is typically open, there are once again different types of "borrowers": companies, industries, institutions, and non-profit companies (Burkett, 2011);
- investors (lenders): the subjects who decide to financially support a project by assuming the risks inherent in each investment against an inevitable, expected return (Ordanini et al., 2011).

Faced with the great difficulties in accessing credit caused by the economic-financial crisis, combined with the increasingly easy access to the Internet by individuals, the evolution of crowdfunding has been rapid as this phenomenon is considered an alternative, dedicated tool to finding financial sources: a new funding model that runs parallel to traditional financing channels. Many believe the development is the so-called credit crunch or a significant drop in credit supply by banks, especially for small and medium-sized enterprises. The Anglo-Saxon market, for example, recorded a substantial increase in participation in crowdlending about the reduction in bank loans offered in the post-financial crisis period of 2008 (De Luca & Lucido, 2019). Suffice it to say that in 2008, Barack Obama also used crowdfunding as a way of financing to support his electoral campaign, obtaining about 137 million dollars.

In addition to these financial advantages, the European Commission in 2015 identified others of a non-financial nature. Crowdfunding:

- it offers the possibility to test if others share the trust in the project and appreciate its value;
- helps to obtain other forms of financing for a given project;
- it caters to a vast audience of people (the crowd), some of whom may have valuable industry experience and knowledge, thus offering feedback at no cost;
- it is a powerful marketing tool and an effective way to present a new product, a new company, or its expansion, focusing directly on the people who are likely to be customers.

The European Commission has also identified several potential risks that crowdfunding should manage:

- there is no guarantee that the company will reach the set objective of the fundraising;
- the idea of the project becomes public domain;
- the costs that some forms of crowdfunding require could be underestimated;
- due to the continuous legislative evolution of the phenomenon, there could be a possible violation of the law;
- care should be taken not to run into fraudulent platforms.

The characteristics of real estate crowdfunding are similar to those of general crowdfunding, except for the platform's goal: to finance real estate projects available online through electronic media.

Each REC project can be used to acquire, lease, or total or partially renovate existing buildings and purchase raw land (Marchand, 2015).

The actors involved are also the same as in general crowdfunding: the promoter of the project, which can be a company or an individual who proposes the idea and/or project to be financed ("the entrepreneur"); investors (individuals or companies) who put in money to support the idea; the platform "that brings the parties together to launch the idea" (Baker, 2015).

In light of these elements, therefore, the REC can be defined as a set of efforts made by entrepreneurs to collect financial resources from a crowd of investors (private or corporate, accredited or not) via an electronic platform to finance various real estate projects, which may have the objective of acquiring, leasing, or relocating existing buildings in whole or in part or purchasing raw land.

Before the start of the project, a due diligence period familiar to any investment is envisaged, during which it is verified whether the company and the project are financially able to comply with the repayment conditions in the medium-long term. One of the main differences between crowdfunding and investments made through traditional channels is the time for approval of projects. "A process that normally takes several months to initiate and finalize has, with platforms, become a streamlined process" (Baker, 2015) as now the same process takes weeks, days, or even hours. Cohen (2016) reveals the importance of this feature, stating that the speed of execution in a real estate transaction is instrumental not only in competing and in winning a deal.

The use of the REC has also introduced a revolutionary method for investing in this sector with the dematerialization of real estate investments. A personal visit to the property was essential for engaging in this project a few years ago. Today, investors are advised to invest based only on the information advertised on the platforms. With real estate crowdfunding, it is sufficient to "browse" offers on a website and support or sell shares in property with a couple of clicks (Schwartz, 2016).

The REC is very similar to a REIT in investment portfolio management control as there is no need to manage the property in both cases physically. Despite this, there are significant differences in transparency: in the REIT, the trustee decides which property to buy and which property to sell,

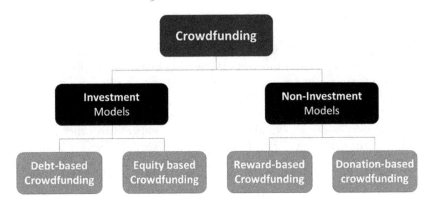

Fig. 5.2 The types of crowdfunding. Source: Querci (2014), "Financial crowdfunding, a new tool for SMEs"

while in the REC, it is the investor who decides which investments to make. The platform discloses all the characteristics of the project on the website, including photos of the asset, reports prepared by analysts, or other relevant corporate strategic documents. The lender can monitor the results after the investment, as the platform provides specific updates on transactions and P2P lending.

According to the European Crowdfunding Network and Querci (2014), there are mainly four types of crowdfunding: Lending-based, Equity-based, Reward-based, and Donation-based (Fig. 5.2).

The lending-based model, called social lending or peer-to-peer lending, falls within crowdfunding. The latter is defined as:

Definition "the model in which lenders and borrowers sign (directly or indirectly) a debt contract, with which the former provides a sum of money and the latter undertakes to repay the capital (almost always increased by a rate of interest) in a given time frame. The subjects financed are families, non-profit associations, and small/medium-sized enterprises (SMEs). At the same time, the investors are generally single subjects, companies offering asset management services, institutional investors or banks." (Bofondi, 2017)

It can therefore be considered an online micro-loan system, directly between individuals, allowing disintermediation in the loan disbursement process (Carignani & Gemmo, 2007). Private individuals usually address the request for a loan to other individuals who, in most cases, do not represent professional investors (Borello et al., 2014). This loan is disbursed without a financial intermediary but through online platforms that make it possible to meet small savers looking for a profitable investment and other subjects in need of funds. P2P lending compared to other known forms of crowdfunding is characterized by the fact that the direct remuneration for the investor is given by the interest paid based on the capital lent and the risk of the loan granted (Caratelli et al., 2016).

There are three actors: lender, applicant, and the intermediary; the latter, represented by the platform, puts lenders in direct contact with loan applicants through an automated computer system.

The main features of P2P lending can be summarized as follows:

- greater flexibility of interest rates;
- obtaining a loan after a bank refused to grant it;
- the size of the loans can vary considerably and thus meet most needs. The minimum lending threshold is shallow, which encourages a large audience of lenders to participate;
- loan repayment through direct payments to the platform, which then distributes the related shares to investors.

In the real estate sector, P2P lending is generally granted on properties whose intended use must concern either newly built apartments or existing houses. The type of activity that can be financed impacts the risk assumed by investors.

The financial solutions offered by P2P platforms in the real estate sector can range from the short term (typically 12–18 months) to the medium to long term (e.g., three to five years). Borrowers can choose between fixed and variable rates under monthly to quarterly payments, or the financing solution can allow the amount of interest at the loan's repayment time (Boppart et al., 2016).

The main risk to which real estate P2P lending investors are exposed is the possibility that the project/builder will fail. However, this risk can be mitigated by the prospect of recovering the initial capital through the collateral of the property (Qi & Yang, 2009).

5.2.1   Object and Operation of P2P Lending

As described in the previous paragraph, P2P lending consists of the direct loan of money between private individuals (P2P consumer) or businesses (P2P business), where an online service combines lenders with borrowers. It has become a new financial management tool for investors interested in high yields in the face of increased risks they expose themselves and for borrowers who cannot receive loans through traditional credit channels (Qian & Hu, 2019).

The innovation of these channels compared to traditional credit intermediaries consists in the possibility of having a loan agreement directly concluded between third parties and customers of the same platform. It is, therefore, a sort of "collective loan" (Bank of Italy, 2016), thanks to the interaction between a plurality of subjects who direct financial resources, through a digital platform, to the applicants for funds. The venue, therefore, has the function of a marketplace, that is, a direct telematic meeting point between surplus and deficit units.

Operation

In the first phase, the borrower (a company or an individual) submits his application for a loan after registering on the online platform (so-called marketplace). Depending on his economic-financial reliability (the so-called creditworthiness), he is offered an interest rate which varies according to his rating (the lower the rating, the higher the rate applied). The first security check that the debtor must pass to access a P2P lending platform concerns the release of personal information: date of birth to determine that the subject is of age, an actual bank account number, or the Social Security number.

If the borrower accepts the interest rate proposal, his request is entered into the marketplace. Now that all the elements are available to choose how to place their liquidity through the platform, lenders can invest capital by choosing from the risk-return profiles. The applicant for the loan receives money (by bank transfer directly to his account) only when his application has received the number of shares necessary to cover the entire sum requested. Should sum as the whole not be reached within the established times, the claims promised by the lenders will be returned to them.

Lenders are generally investors of various kinds: consumers, banks, institutional investors, or asset management companies. On the other hand, the borrowers are households, small and medium-sized enterprises, and non-profit associations.

So what do P2P lending platforms do? The media generally have the following characteristics:

- They collect the loan applications and analyze the information released by the borrowers;
- they select potential borrowers by evaluating their creditworthiness and assign them a score, called credit score rating, usually based on a model called FICO (from Fair Isaac Corporation), which represents their degree of risk;
- they allow each lender to finance many subjects based on their risk/ return preferences;
- they manage payments between lenders and borrowers in a more or less direct way (depending on whether the platform uses a third party or not);
- implement debt collection actions if the borrower becomes insolvent;
- they receive commissions, which generally vary between 0.25% and 2.5% of the loan amount.

P2P lending can also be distinguished based on the different borrowers they target (Fig. 5.3):

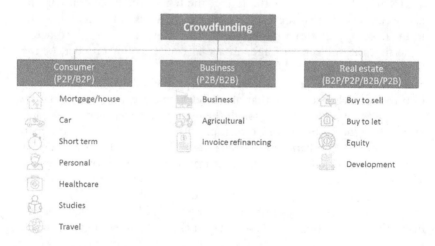

Fig. 5.3 The different types of borrowers in crowdfunding

- Consumer Loans: loans aimed mainly at consumers; consequently, the main types of loans requested in these platforms are part of consumer credit;
- Business Loans: loans primarily aimed at SMEs;
- Real Estate Loans: loans secured by real estate.

A fundamental aspect of P2P lending is determining the interest rate, which can be fixed through an auction process or directly from the platform (Amrein et al., 2015).

The auction-based process starts after the borrower fills out the loan application, specifying the maximum interest rate he is willing to accept. The lender determines the minimum interest rate he is ready to invest. Once the application has been uploaded to the site, a sort of auction is generated in which the lenders propose and offer various interest rates and the amount they are willing to invest in the project. The auction ends when the lenders' offer exceeds the amount requested by the borrower. Lenders know that offering a higher interest rate implies a lower chance of being chosen as the auction is generally won by the lenders who have shown the lowest interest rates.

Once the lowest interest rates have been selected, the average interest rate is calculated and then proposed to the borrower; he can choose whether to accept it or not.

Usually, the platforms that use this auction process (e.g., Zopa and Prosper) are based on the principle of all-or-nothing, as they foresee that if a project does not attract sufficient financiers in a certain period (i.e., until the auction does not expire), the loan application should be removed from the system. All previous bids should be canceled.

In reality, this auction procedure is used less and less, not only due to the element of difficulty it creates for investors in choosing the interest rate (often, the average investor does not know this method of action or does not have time to participate in the auction), but also due to the higher costs that platforms incur using this model.

In the second case, the platform chooses the interest rate directly. The match between supply and demand is automatic as the platform proposes an interest rate for each risk category. Investors know what interest rate to expect (Milne & Parboteeah, 2016). The platform also provides that the fundraiser does not have a precise amount to reach, so the goal is simply to raise as much money as possible (Zhao et al., 2017).

5.2.2   The Opportunities Offered by P2P Lending

Technological development has facilitated disintermediation by allowing operators to access more efficient and immediate communication channels while generating better service for lenders and borrowers (Milne & Parboteeah, 2016).

The success of lending-based crowdfunding, which has led to exponential growth worldwide, is primarily due to a series of competitive advantages over traditional credit intermediaries. These advantages fall into two categories: economic advantages; operational benefits.

The Economic Benefits

On the lender's side, the platforms introduce the possibility of investing in a new asset class belonging to loans (Bofondi, 2017), benefiting portfolio diversification. Households and institutional investors have always been able to invest directly in consumer loans and only indirectly in loans to small and medium-sized enterprises through securitization transactions. Thanks to P2P platforms, households and institutional investors can invest directly in any asset class to diversify their portfolios and not face securitization costs (Aveni, 2015).

In terms of cost, online platforms make it possible to reduce the fixed costs that a traditional bank is usually forced to face (just think of the cost of maintaining a network of branches), allowing lenders to obtain a high return on their investment (Kirby & Worner, 2014). Deloitte (2016) highlights three main cost factors that, in general, affect financing:

- the cost of financing;
- operating costs;
- how risk is "priced".

Generally, to grant a loan, a bank must first be equipped with deposits, equity, and liquidity reserves; hence the existence of direct costs on financing and liquidity (such as interest rates), costs to develop and implement services offered to depositors, without counting the costs of managing a network of branches or marketing costs. On the other hand, the platform has a more streamlined structure; therefore, despite the need to bear costs related to the management of the platform rather than aimed at marketing activities, they will not have to face expenses associated with the management of current accounts or branches.

In terms of return, the study conducted by Morse (2015) on the data provided by the US platforms (Lending Club and Prosper) shows that the net return for investors averaged between 7% and 8% in the period from 2007 to 2014. In the same period, the return on ABS related to consumer credit securitization transactions (according to the Barclays Capital Fixed ABS Index) was 4% (around 3% less than that of crowdlending platforms). Meanwhile, corporate bonds (according to data provided by Morningstar on the Barclays US Corporate Investment Grade Index) returned 5.49%. This could explain why the phenomenon of P2P lending has also met with great success on the side of investors (especially institutional ones).

Another advantage is given by the facilitation of access to credit (in traditional channels) often denied to those subjects considered "more at risk", especially for companies in the start-up phase that, due to an almost or utterly non-existent credit history, find it difficult to obtain financing from a traditional credit institution (De Luca & Lucido, 2019). For SMEs, the use of debt remains essential. When banks are reluctant to grant loans, especially if the external economic and financial environment is not the most favorable and the regulation is increasingly stringent, alternative sources can be vital. P2P lending has therefore become one of the most widespread alternative sources of credit and one of the clearest examples of modern financial innovation.

The Operational Advantages

As previously stated, the technology can guarantee a whole series of operational advantages. By attributing the credit risk to investors, the platforms do not have to hold any liquidity reserves and are subject to less stringent regulations than banking regulations. Furthermore, they can maintain their profitability even in the event of an increase in the cost of capital and grant loans even to high-risk borrowers (Nash & Beardsley, 2015).

The technological innovations used in the lending process typical of platforms are potentially scalable in that they may not increase as exponentially as the growing volumes of crowdlending (Perkins, 2018). The operational advantages could therefore grow in step with the development of the phenomenon itself.

The computerization of all the phases also allows a considerable gain in terms of time. The heavy infrastructures typical of traditional credit institutions are a source of both higher costs and lower efficiency in terms of speed of completion, forcing them to adapt operating models to technological progress constantly. On the other hand, the platforms use almost entirely mechanical structures and processes that allow processing loan requests up to the actual credit disbursement in a short time.

The same rating and scoring systems implemented by the platforms are subject to particular attention due to their accuracy. While traditional intermediaries use models based more on the past credit performance of debtors, crowdlending media exploit a more comprehensive range of information (from simple monthly cash flows and outflows to specific activity on social networks), thanks to sophisticated Machine Learning algorithms (ML) and Big Data Analytics techniques (Sciarrone Alibrandi et al., 2019).

These innovative methods are characterized by solid flexibility and the ability to analyze massive datasets, with all the pros and cons that come with them. However, the empirical evidence demonstrates that ML-type models show a better out-of-sample forecasting capacity than traditional models, the relationship between the dependent variable (risk) and the explanatory ones (Branzoli & Supino, 2020).

5.2.3   Risks and Disadvantages of P2P Lending

The main risks associated with all the players in peer-to-peer lending have been identified by the European Banking Authority (2015) and concern:

Credit Risk

This risk can also be attributed to the loss of the debtor's capital in insolvency, as the investment in unsecured loans is without guarantees from P2P platforms. The lender assumes the entire risk of default of the applicant. The platforms do not operate like banks and do not take the risk directly. To try to remedy this problem, they can provide for loan mechanisms called "one to many bases", in the sense that they provide for a mandatory diversification of the investment over several loans so as to reduce individual exposure; or, they can adopt a business model that allows them to turn to outside companies for debt collection.

The Risk of Fraud

The risk of fraud is determined by certain factors, such as fraudulent conduct by the debtor and the platform's low-security standards, which can lead to theft and/or abuse of digital identity. Regarding the debtor's fraudulent conduct, it should be emphasized that peer-to-peer loans are linked to the same risks that traditional entities face: identity theft, consumer privacy, and money laundering. The fact that most platforms operate on websites and the Internet leads to a greater likelihood of fraud precisely because of the Internet's anonymity (Chaffee & Geoffrey, 2012). To prevent this behavior, the platform acquires information concerning the debtor's identity and economic and financial status, forbidding access to the site in case of classification as a potential fraudulent counterpart. However, platforms don't put the same effort into evaluating loan counterparties but often simply try to comply with anti-money laundering laws (Kirby & Worner, 2014).

Liquidity Risk
In a peer-to-peer loan, liquidity risk is related to the inability to liquidate an investment before maturity once it has been entered into the platform. Only some platforms allow the lender to transfer and/or liquidate his credit position in advance: it is an operation that takes place within the site under certain conditions and contractual constraints, thus making the investment illiquid and blocking the investor until upon expiry (so-called locked-in). Some peer-to-peer lending platforms offer a secondary market for investors to facilitate liquidating all or part of their loan portfolios. In other cases, the media can buy loans from investors and then securitize them.

Operational and Legal Risks
Operational risks are determined by errors or malfunctions of the platform caused by technology, people, and processes. These risks arise if the platform does not have an adequate organizational system and the technological system is inappropriate. However, these risks must also be added to those of a macroeconomic nature that influence the existence and return of this new form of investment.
    Legal and operational risks concern:

- the regulation to be applied;
- relationship management, in particular in the event of complaints;
- the management of financial flows deriving from investments;
- the allocation of repayment flows from debtors.

The risks are associated with inadequate or misleading information.

Borrowers usually benefit from the lack of transparency they offer to creditors, and creditors certainly cannot expect to know all the characteristics of borrowers. The imbalance of information between subjects can cause inefficiency within the markets and develop the phenomenon of "adverse selection." Lenders could give their money to issues that cannot pay them back, which is why the existence of these information asymmetries can contribute to making bad decisions.

The anonymous nature of the peer-to-peer market, therefore, exposes the lender to a substantial lack of information, and he must base his decisions on unverified information or, in any case deriving from risk models decided by the platforms themselves. In the real estate market, there are various forms of information asymmetry, but, in general, they can be divided into information asymmetries relating to the characteristics of the property itself; information asymmetries related to the market conditions in which the property is traded. Most non-professional investors cannot distinguish profitable REC projects from unprofitable ones, that is, whether an entrepreneur or project is good or bad is primarily hidden information from lenders (Tomboc, 2013).

The Risk of Money Laundering
The risk of money laundering is linked to the possibility that investors not correctly verified by the platform can use these platforms to start fraudulent activities or launder money. Some solutions to eliminate or minimize the risk could be linked to appropriate assessments of customers, which aim to acquire more information such as addresses, creditworthiness, and criminal record of the investor.

So what are the main risks for lenders?

As highlighted, most platforms never internalize credit risk but transfer it permanently to investors. This could incentivize the same media to guarantee the disbursement of riskier loans for higher remuneration.

The risks increase when financing uncollateralized loans (without guarantees). In the event of default, relying on the platform and specialized debt collection entities is necessary, making the process particularly burdensome for the lender and with little probability of success.

It is also appropriate to consider the presence of information asymmetries that make it difficult to distinguish "good" projects from "bad" ones, given the scarce availability of quantitative information provided, and which can therefore mislead lenders (Vallée & Zeng, 2019).

Another risk is the possibility that the platform does not assume any responsibility in the event of bankruptcy (Kirby & Worner, 2014).

The absence of a secondary market can be an additional risk factor, making it particularly difficult for fund lenders to liquidate their investments before maturity.

So what are the main risks for borrowers?

One of the main risks for these subjects concerns the possibility of undergoing identity theft to ensure the obtainment of a loan. Since there is no formal interview, the platform cannot verify the borrower's actual origin information.

Other possible risks are then highlighted by the study conducted by the GAO (2011). Among these, we find the possible presence of opaque and unclear contractual clauses, opportunistic and discriminatory behaviors, and the abuse of improper practices in the servicing activity by the operators to the detriment of the borrowers.

5.2.4   Business Models

Different ways to match borrowers' requests with lenders' interests perfectly exist. A first distinction can be made between diffused model and the direct model.

In the first case, the platform actively works by selecting loan applications, collecting money from various investors, and deciding how to sort the funds received on multiple loans. By operating in this way, the platform guarantees a diversification of investments and simultaneously tries to satisfy all loan requests in a short time. In the direct model, on the other hand, each investor decides which project to finance, often ensuring that not all borrowers reach the requested amounts and thus obtain the loan (Omarini, 2018).

Kirby and Worner (2014) were the first to outline what is considered the "basic" models of the crowdlending phenomenon by defining three types:

- Client Segregated Account model;
- Notary model;
- Guaranteed Return model.

The Financial Stability Board (2017) then defined two further business models:

- The Balance Sheet Model
- Invoice Trading Model

In the Client Segregated Account model, the platform is limited to facilitating the meeting between lenders and borrowers. Starting from the assessment of creditworthiness (the borrower is analyzed on the riskiness of the project, the lender is assessed based on the risk he intends to assume and, therefore, based on his expected return), the platform makes a list available to lenders potential projects in which to invest by giving them the possibility of choice through an auction mechanism (previously described). The loan is disbursed only when the amount requested by the borrower is reached.

The peculiarity of the process is that the funds, both of the employers and the borrowers, are shown in a separate balance sheet from the platform, and the latter cannot operate there directly. The funds converge in the so-called client segregated account and remain entirely unrelated to the possible failure of the platform.

The platform is solely tasked with managing incoming and outgoing flows and their accounting against a commission.

The adoption of this model guarantees equity separation between the platform and its users, with the consequent absence of the medium of direct exposure to credit risk, which remains the responsibility of the lenders. The lenders can claim their credit rights exclusively toward the subjects financed by them if they are insolvent or late in payments (Fig. 5.4).

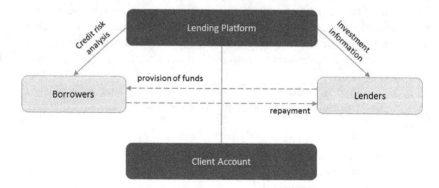

Fig. 5.4 The business model of the Client Segregated Account model. Source: Financial Stability Board (2017), "Fintech Credit: Market Structure, Business Models and Financial Stability Implications"

The Notary model provides for the participation of the platform in the matching phase between lenders and borrowers and in the publication of the loan request if the creditworthiness assessment is successful. The funds are not collected by the platform but by a custodian bank that proceeds with the disbursement of the loan according to the "all or nothing" method, that is, only when the total amount requested is reached.

From the study conducted by the United States Government Accountability Office (GAO) (2011) on the Prosper and Lending Club platforms, it emerges that the custodian bank sells the credit to the forum in exchange for the amount obtained from the so-called notes that investors subscribe based on the sums paid in favor of the loan. The "notes" themselves are therefore nothing more than securities representing the part attributable to the investor concerning the amount of credit disbursed. Furthermore, some jurisdictions are attributed to the nature of transferable securities (Caratelli et al., 2016).

This mechanism ensures that the credit risk is not assumed by the custodian bank or the platform itself. Still, it is transferred only to the lenders following the subscription of the "notes."

As in the Client Segregated Account model, any insolvency of the financed parties does not affect the platform's stability. The individual lender does not remain without protection: the platform, through the credit recovery companies (at the expense of the borrower and the lender), can solicit the payment of the sums owed by the insolvent debtor.

The Notary Model is the most used solution in the United States, for example, by the Prosper and Lending Club platforms (Fig. 5.5).

The Guaranteed Return model emphasizes even more the role of the platform as an intermediary as it can directly disburse the loans using the money raised by the lenders, guaranteeing them a specific rate of return (hence the name "Guaranteed Return") established based on the rating class assigned to each project.

It is, therefore, the platform that deals with both the screening phase of potential borrowers and the credit origination phase, identifying which projects to finance and under what conditions. The same manage the investors' money and collects the borrowers' periodic installments of the borrowers thus assuming the credit risk (unlike in other business models).

Therefore, it is crucial that the platform's remuneration guarantees at least the coverage of management costs and establishes a guarantee fund

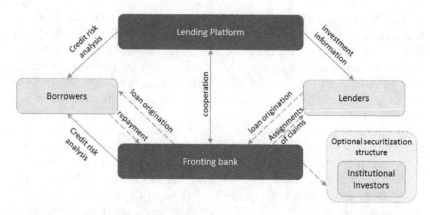

Fig. 5.5 The business model of the Notary model. Source: Financial Stability Board (2017), "Fintech Credit: Market Structure, Business Models and Financial Stability Implications"

for investors in case of delays or non-payments by borrowers (Sciarrone Alibrandi et al., 2019).

According to the analysis of Kirby and Worner (2014), the model can be broken down into two variants. The first involves using direct channels and formal interviews with potential borrowers to acquire information to determine creditworthiness (for this reason, it is also known as the "Offline Guaranteed Return Model"). The second phase then provides that the loans that can be financed are published on the online platform, leaving investors the opportunity to make an offer.

The country that has favored this model most of all is China: the over-supply by investors has led to the need for direct contact with potential borrowers, which is crucial for the attractiveness of these alternative forms of financing.

Another less common variant involves using an automated system implemented by the platform, which collects the sums of money deposited by investors and distributes them to the various financing projects according to specific criteria. The platform then guarantees lenders a minimum remuneration that can grow over time at a predetermined rate (Fig. 5.6).

In the Balance Sheet Model, platforms originate loans and keep them on their balance sheets; this model is developed in Australia, Canada, and the United States. This development is mainly because lenders have increasingly relied on sources of debt capital. The fundamental difference

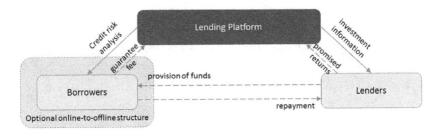

Fig. 5.6 The business model of the Guaranteed Return model. Source: Financial Stability Board (2017), "Fintech Credit: Market Structure, Business Models and Financial Stability Implications"

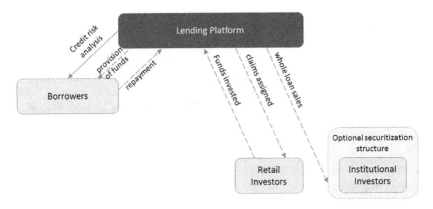

Fig. 5.7 The business model of the Balance Sheet Model. Source: Financial Stability Board (2017), "Fintech Credit: Market Structure, Business Models and Financial Stability Implications"

between the Balance Sheet Model and the Notary Model is that the platform uses its resources to issue debt securities when repurchases the credit disbursed by the fronting bank.

In this case, the platform remunerates itself through the interest margin, that is, the difference between the interest income and the interest expense that the loans generate (Fig. 5.7).

Finally, some platforms deal with the discount of commercial invoices or invoice trading. The platforms that use the Invoice Trading Model aim to address start-ups and SMEs, offering more flexible services than traditional operators and factoring companies (in the recourse mode). The platforms take care of automatically processing invoices and providing liquidity and financing to debtors.

5.3   The Main National and International Players in P2P Lending

The leading players considered first movers, that is, the countries that first moved in the context of P2P lending platforms, are England and the United States.

Since 2005, the number of companies operating in the sector has multiplied considerably in England, followed by the USA, Europe, Asia, and South America (early followers). Italy, Spain, and France are instead considered the late-mover countries.

The idea of disintermediation of the loan disbursement process was born in 2005 with the creation of the first platform called Zopa. Those who rely on this platform must meet some minimum requirements: British residence, minimum age of 20, and an income stream of at least 12,000 pounds. The platform provides loans between 1000 and 25,000 pounds, ranging from one, two, three, four, or five years. In 2013 it expanded the audience of debtors by introducing sole proprietorships that reach 0.01% with loans equal to 1 million pounds. Before granting the loan, Zopa provides a meticulous internal verification process regarding helpful information on the debtor; in the event of the debtor's insolvency, the platform offers the debt collection procedure at the expense of the debtor with the help of agencies specializing in the collection of late payments. In this regard, Zopa uses the Safeguard fund, fed by the commissions paid by the debtors at the time of signing the loan to intervene in the event of its default.

Another British player in the sector is Ratesetter, founded in 2010 to develop in the international market. According to the founders, "Ratesetter's business is based on the reengineering of the intermediation process between creditors and debtors; therefore, extensive use is made of the services offered by the banks, but focused on certain phases of the process such as the screening of the debtor's solvency." This platform uses a credit recovery fund; based on the applicant's creditworthiness, it applies different rates and commissions and, in the event of late payment, involves a new deadline (in agreement with the debtor) against a penalty to be paid by the borrower.

As for the United States market (we will make just a few hints here), Prosper and Lending Club stand out among the leading platforms. Prosper was the first to appear in the market above (the year 2006) but held the second position in terms of volumes. In fact, since 2006, it has generated volumes of over USD6 billion. Lending Club remains the most developed platform in the American market and holds the primacy of the largest platform in the world, which has grown to go public with an IPO that began in 2014 on the New York Stock Exchange. Both platforms divide their users according to their solvency, classifying them from AA (low risk, low return) to HR (high risk, high return) and adopting a notary business model.

In Europe, except in the UK, the phenomenon has expanded more modestly in terms of volume, but not in terms of time: in Germany in 2007, Auxmoney was founded, in Italy, 2007 it opened a Zopa branch, and in France in 2014 was created Lendix and in Latvia in 2015 Mintos (Table 5.1).

As for the P2P lending platforms operating in the real estate sector, the undisputed leaders are Germany, and the United Kingdom, followed by Switzerland and France (Table 5.2).

In Italy, the REC market is developing very rapidly, and the financing volumes are growing year after year (Fig. 5.8).

Table 5.1 Best crowdfunding platforms in Europe in 2020

Rank	Platform	Return (ROI)	Minimum investment	BuyBack guarantee	Bonus	Investment type
1	Mintos	11%	€5	Yes	1%	Business/Consumer
2	Fast Invest	12.5%	€1	Yes	–	Consumer
3	Crowdestor	18%	€50	No	0.5%	Business (company, Crypto, restaurant)
4	Bulkestate	14.8%	€50	No	–	Real estate
5	Estateguru	11.3%	€50	No	0.5%	Real estate
6	NEO Finance	12%	€10	Yes	€25	Consumer
7	PeerBerry	12%	€10	Yes	–	Business, real estate
8	ROBOCASH	12%	€10	Yes	–	Business, consumer
9	SWAPER	12%	€10	Yes	–	Consumer
10	Viainvest	11%	€10	Yes	–	Consumer
11	Summer crowd	16%	€100	No	–	Real estate
12	FinBee	18%	€5	No	–	Business, consumer
13	Housers	8%	€50	No	€25	Real estate

Source: crowdfunding-platforms.com, Elaborated by the authors

Table 5.2   Best RECs in Europe for 2021

Rank	Platform	Foundation year	ROI (2020)	Minimum investment	Projects in
1	SummerGuru	2013	12%	€50.00	Estonia, Latvia, Lithuania, Spain, Finland, Germany
2	CrowdProperty	2014	8%	£500.00	UK
3	Crowdestate	2014	17%	€100.00	Multiple countries
4	Raizers	2014	12%	€1000.00	France, Switzerland, Benelux countries
5	Bulkestate	2016	18%	€50.00	Baltic states
6	Property Partner	2015	11%	€50.00	UK
7	Blend Network	2016	12%	£1000.00	North Ireland, Scotland, England
8	Rendity	2015	7%	€1000.00	Austria, Germany
9	Kuflink	2016	7%	£1000.00	UK
10	Nordstreet	2018	11%	€100.00	Lithuania

Source: ampleinvest.com

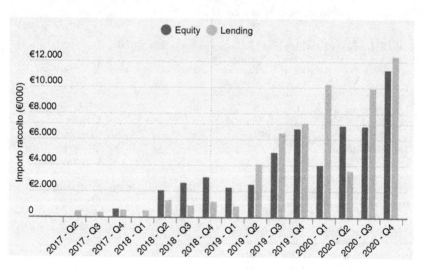

Fig. 5.8   The volumes of equity and lending crowdfunding in Italy from 2017 to 2020. Source: www.crowdfundingbuzz.it

Fig. 5.9 The risk/return of debt securities of equity and lending crowdfunding platforms. Source: p2p marketdata.com

A 9.5% gross per annum can be expected from lending-type platforms. On the other hand, when investing in an equity-type platform, the average expected return is 12% gross per annum. The risk is proportional to the return and depends on the seniority of the debt securities one invests (Fig. 5.9).

In the following paragraphs we will proceed with a minor focus on the functioning of debt and equity crowdfunding, the main types used to finance real estate projects and which have recently been regulated by the European Commission (in early March 2018) through the Regulation on European Crowdfunding Service Providers (ECSP) for Business, that is the Regulation on European crowdfunding service providers for businesses (ECSP). Furthermore, according to CrowdfundingBuzz statistics data from November 2020, more than 29 million euros were raised for real estate lending crowdfunding and more than 26.5 million euros for equity in the real estate sector, far exceeding the numbers registered in 2019.

5.4   Debt-Crowdfunding

The 2019 Finance Law has extended the operations of equity crowdfunding platforms, making it possible to finance small and medium-sized enterprises through portals, including through the underwriting of bonds and/

or debt financial instruments. In 2019, the equity crowdfunding platforms were therefore authorized, which until then were the only ones that could operate as intermediaries for the collection of risk capital, to also operate as intermediaries for the collection of loans through bonds and debt financial instruments—Issued by small and medium-sized enterprises (so-called debt crowdfunding). In this way, the companies that fall within the provisions of the law, for example, can place mini-bonds through portals authorized by CONSOB. In the case of debt crowdfunding, the investor lends a certain amount of money and receives a bill issued by the platform.

The investor lends a certain amount of money and receives a bill issued by the platform.

Non "accredited" investors should be aware of the different lending structures that can be used on these platforms. Suppose the investor opts for a senior debt structure (Fig. 5.9). In that case, the loan on the platform is secured by placing a tier one lien on the property, offering lenders high protection in the event of a debtor's insolvency.

A recent innovation in the market was introducing the so-called bridging loan option (Matejka, 2016), considered a short-term debt, as the loan is due in less than a year, against high-interest rates. However, a bridging loan is risky for investors as there is no guarantee that the proposed plan to repay the debt will be fulfilled in the short term (Goins, 2014).

Operation

The companies describe in detail the requirements of their loan (amount requested, business objectives, purpose of the loan) and send their financial data to a crowdfunding or peer-to-peer lending platform. The terms of the loan, such as minimum investment limit, suitability of the investor profile, loan repayment APR and any other details, will be decided and defined by the platform as part of its due diligence. Depending on the loan amount, the company will be required to provide personal or company assets guarantees.

The platform then advertises the investment opportunity through its website and other online channels. Loan repayments generally begin within a month or two of the company receiving the loan.

The main advantages deriving from this crowdfunding model are:

- reduction of the time that a borrower would spend waiting for a loan to be approved by relying on a traditional credit institution;
- it is considered a low-risk investment as the debt has collateral;

- The company collects capital to finance a product or service without selling the shares (shares) of its company but by keeping the entire ownership.

The Risks
Lenders can lose some or all of their investment if a company cannot make repayments or go into liquidation. In liquidation, the lenders are treated like any other creditor and may or may not receive the proceeds from any assets the liquidators sell. However, as loans are generally granted against some form of collateral, it is considered a low-risk investment.

5.5 EQUITY CROWDFUNDING

Equity-based crowdfunding—more recently introduced on the international scene and organically regulated for the first time by Italian law with art. 30 law decree n. 179/2012, the "growth bis" decree, converted into law no. 221 of 17 December 2012—identifies the widespread collection of risk capital by innovative start-ups through online portals.

With the Decree, the definition of "innovative startup" was introduced into our system, which art. 25 of the decree defines as "a capital company, also incorporated in a cooperative form [...] whose shares or quotas are not listed on a regulated market or a multilateral trading system."

This legislation provides administrative, fiscal, and bankruptcy benefits for innovative start-ups.

Specifically, to be defined as an innovative start-up, a company must meet the following requirements:

- be established and have operated for no more than 60 months;
- be resident in Italy or one of the Member States of the European Union;
- the total annual production value must not exceed €5 million;
- must not distribute or have distributed profits;
- it must have as its exclusive or prevailing corporate purpose the development, production, and marketing of innovative products or services with high technological value;
- it must not have been established due to a corporate merger, spin-off, or following the sale of a company or company branch.

In addition, it must meet at least one of the following criteria:

- Incur expenses in research and development equal to or greater than 15% of the more significant amount between the cost and the value of production;
- to employ at least one-third doctoral students, doctorates, or researchers, or a percentage equal to or greater than two-third of the workforce must have a master's degree;
- be the owner, custodian, or licensee of at least one industrial technology.

In Italy, the spread of equity crowdfunding has been slow. First of all, this form of financing was initially envisaged only for innovative start-ups, and this discouraged the "crowd" as it involved the funding of mere ideas, which not even a highly professional investor with a very high-risk profile would have taken into consideration. It was common to think that the ideas were financed with the personal investment of the partners, the bank loan and possibly with some small public contribution to encourage innovation (Lerro, 2013). An attempt was made to fill this gap through the amendment of the 2018 Regulation in which it is envisaged that the subjects qualified to submit offers on the portals are SMEs; innovative start-up companies; innovative SMEs; the collective investment scheme ("UCI") which invests mainly in SMEs; corporations that invest primarily in SMEs.

A further cause of slow diffusion of the model lies in the too-cumbersome system imposed by Regulation no. 18592 of the CONSOB, which entailed a series of preliminary formalities for the platforms, such as, for example, finding a necessarily banking partner.

So the initial failure of equity crowdfunding is ascribed to the initial legislative choice to focus only on innovative start-ups, which of all companies are the most difficult to understand and evaluate and those on which the information asymmetry.

Operation

The equity crowdfunding applied to the real estate sector provides that the online investment is made directly in the special purpose company that aims to carry out a specific real estate project. This means that the investor buys a share of the company. In this case, the reward for the cash contribution consists of a certain number of corporate equity securities and, consequently, of the set of property and administrative rights incorporated in the securities themselves (Thomas, 2014). The shareholding in the

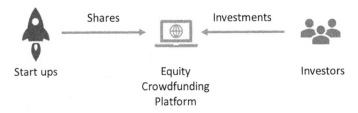

Fig. 5.10 How equity crowdfunding works. Source: Authors' elaboration

company entails administrative and property rights, such as the right to receive future dividends and the opportunity to realize capital gains from the sale of shareholdings to third parties.

Adherents, therefore, make a real investment if and only if the collection is completed, that is, if the issuer receives within a specific deadline several offers such as to cover the entire required capital. If the collection is successful, the lenders become shareholders of the company to all intents and purposes (Filotto, 2016) (Fig. 5.10).

Equity crowdfunding is, therefore, an attractive way to invest in real estate (Schweizer & Barkley, 2017). These platforms are structured differently from the others: the SPV is used for each real estate project. This entity, managed by the platform, assumes the ongoing management of the real estate assets, controlling profits and costs (Goins, 2014). The crowd of investors buys shares in this company, and, as shareholders of the SPV, they are entitled to receive a percentage of the rental income or profits from the sale, if any. It should be noted that today, there are different investment options: common stocks, preferred stocks, mezzanine debt, bridging loans, and so on. This platform, prevalent in Southeast Asia, allows developers to list investment opportunities via the Internet, connecting investors with developers seeking funding. However, these platforms are risky as they are hardly subject to the investor's legal information or protection obligations.

Equity crowdfunding can offer several benefits to both companies and investors (Vulkan et al., 2016):

– easier access to capital: platforms allow entrepreneurs and companies to show their projects to a more significant number of potential investors compared to conventional forms of raising money;

- less pressure on management: the involvement of a large number of investors means that power is not concentrated around a particular group of shareholders;
- very high returns: you can provide very profitable returns to investors.

The Risks

Anyone wishing to participate in equity crowdfunding must be aware of its risks. Some of these include:

- dilution of capital: since equity crowdfunding is related to the issue of new shares, the share of current shareholders will be diluted;
- High risk of project failure: startups are hazardous businesses. Therefore, there is a high probability that the company will fail;
- low liquidity: potential investors should be aware that securities purchased on equity crowdfunding platforms are highly illiquid. Therefore, the exit options are limited. Just as with traditional venture capital investors, crowdfunding investors may have to wait several years for their investment to pay off;
- fraud risk: scammers can use information asymmetries and loopholes in regulations to fool investors. However, the platforms work diligently to verify the information provided by companies seeking funding;
- conflict of interest: the equity crowdfunding platform can create conflicts of interest. For this purpose art. 13 of the CONSOB Regulation establishes a prohibition for the platform manager to formulate recommendations regarding the financial instruments subject to the individual offers, capable of influencing their performance. The managers must ensure that the information and documentation presented by the issuing companies to potential investors are clear, transparent, complete, updated, and accessible for the twelve months following the closing of the offers and, in any case, available for the following five years for those who make the request.

Given the difficulties of smaller companies in accessing private capital, equity crowdfunding, now facilitated by the EU regulation that will come into force on 10 November 2021, appears as a valid alternative to capitalize on the most promising SMEs.

5.6 Conclusion

A recently used option to raise funds among real estate investors is real estate crowdfunding, which involves raising funds to buy properties to sell or rent. The approach has become a viable alternative to traditional methods of raising funds for investments. It brings together small amounts of finance from various investors to finance a real estate or real estate portfolio. As an investor, it is possible to invest the funds through shares or debt instruments in exchange for a specific return obtained from the project (through, e.g., an increase in the value of the asset and its sale or from the rental of the property).

The main attraction of peer-to-peer lending in real estate investments is that it offers small investors the opportunity to participate in real estate projects requiring large investments for a substantial return received.

Whatever the purpose, peer-to-peer lending is increasingly becoming a viable option for raising funds for real estate investment projects. The industry has seen a growing number of crowdfunding investors. A 2019 report by Transparency Market Research indicated that the number of loans issued in crowdfunding increases by 10% per year and the value of transactions by 27.4%. With this growth, the global peer-to-peer lending market is expected to grow to a market value of €900 billion by 2024. In Europe alone (excluding the UK), the crowdfunding sector has grown to 211 billion € of equity loans, 159 in reward loans and 53 in donations.

After all, there are many benefits associated with these types of investments. For borrowers: increase funding sources; allows young real estate companies to get projects started faster; crowdfunding involves direct marketing, which helps promote sponsored real estate business; the company can access valuable feedback from the online crowdfunding community. For investors: it offers the possibility of making short-term investments with high returns; crowdfunding has the advantage of the transparency of transactions as members know exactly where their funds will be invested; it offers the opportunity to diversify your investment across various asset classes and countries.

There are two ways to go for an investment in real estate through crowdfunding: investing in shares or investing with debt instruments.

Lending-based crowdfunding is the most common path for investors as it is easier to invest. In this investment, funds are lent to the property owner against a fixed interest. On the other hand, investing in shares offers higher returns than investing in debt, as through this way, you receive returns based on the property's rental income minus the fees of the crowd-funding platform. The most significant risk associated with this type of investment is that investors own a stake in the property, so they can lose money if the value of the asset falls.

As we have seen, these forms of alternative financing are enjoying great success in Europe, also thanks to the new Regulation (EU) 2020/1503 of 7 October 2020, which will be applied starting from 10 November 2021 and which provides for the creation of a single European market for crowdfunding to promote crowdfunding as an alternative finance tool and to facilitate a more effective allocation of capital within the EU. The license to operate that each platform can obtain from the competent domestic authority is expected to have the value of a passport to operate in all Member States, albeit with the necessary administrative require-ments (articles 12 and 18). The Regulation is also characterized by intro-ducing a series of protections and transparency rules modeled on the MiFID II Directive. Furthermore, always in compliance with the transpar-ency requirements, the European Authority for Financial Instruments and Markets (ESMA) is expected to set up and maintain a public register of crowdfunding service providers (Article 14). Finally, the high accessibility of the sector through web channels and the expected returns (interest is around 10% annually) make this type of alternative investment increasingly enjoyable.

Therefore, lending, equity, and debt crowdfunding constitute innova-tive methods for raising risk and debt capital, the success of which also derives from an ever more significant financial and banking disintermedia-tion and the relative economic advantages consequent to this.

References

Amrein, S., Dietrich, A., Duss, C., & Wernli, R. (2015). *Crowdfunding in the cultural sector.* www.hslu.ch/crowdfunding

Arner, D. W., Barberis, J. N., & Buckley, R. P. (2015). *The evolution of Fintech: A new post-crisis paradigm?* Research Paper No. 2016-62, University of Hong Kong Faculty of Law. https://ssrn.com/abstract=2676553

Aveni, T. (2015, August). New insights into an evolving P2P lending industry: How shifts in roles and risk are shaping the industry. *Positive Planet.*

Baker, C. (2015). Real estate crowdfunding – modern trend or restructured investment model?: Have the SEC's proposed rules on crowdfunding created a closed-market system? *The Journal of Business, Entrepreneurship & The Law,*

Pepperdine University School of Law, 9(1), 21–58. https://digitalcommons. pep-perdine.edu/jbel/vol9/iss1/2/

Bank of Italy. (2016). *Provision containing provisions for the collection of savings by entities other than banks.* Resolution 584/2016.

Baum, A. (2017). *PropTech 3.0: The future of real estate.* Said Business School. http://eureka.sbs.ox.ac.uk/6485/1/122037%20PropTech_FINAL.pdf.

Belezas, F. (2017). *Crowdfunding: Regime Jurídico do Financiamento Colaborativo.* Almedina.

Belleflamme, P., Lambert, T., & Schwienbacher, A. (2013). Crowdfunding: Tapping the right crowd. *Journal of Business Venturing, 29*(5), 585–609. https://papers.ssrn.com/sol3/papers.cfm?abstract_id=1836873

Bofondi, M. (2017). *Lending-based crowdfunding: Opportunities and risks.* Occasional Papers, n. 375, Rome.

Boppart, S., Fries, D., Hasenmeile, F., Huerzeler, F., Kaufmann, P., Luethi, M., Rieder, T., & Waltert, F. (2016). *Banished from paradise.* Swiss Real Estate Market, Credit Suisse.

Borello, G., De Crescenzo, V., & Pichler, F. (2014). Le piattaforme di Financial return crowdfunding nell'Unione europea. *Bancaria,* (12), 77–90.

Bouncken, R. D., Komorek, M., & Kraus, S. (2015). Crowdfunding: The current state of research. *International Business & Economics Research Journal, 14*(2), 407–416.

Branzoli, N., & Supino, I. (2020). *FinTech credit: A critical review of the empirical literature.* Questioni di Economia e Finanza (Occasional Papers), n. 549, Rome.

Burkett, E. (2011). A crowdfunding exemption-online investment crowdfunding and US securities regulation. *Transactions: The Tennessee Journal of Business Law, 13.*

Caratelli, M., Filotto, U., Gibilaro, L., & Mattarocci, G. (2016). The peer-to-peer lending market in the world and the prospects for Italy. *Bancaria, 72*(3), 67–71.

Carignani, A., & Gemmo, V. (2007). Prestiti peer-to-peer: Modelli di business e strategie. *Credito popolare, 14*(3–4), 409–425.

Chaffee, E. C., & Rapp, G. C. (2012). Regulating online peer-to-peer lending in the aftermath of Dodd-Frank: In search of an evolving regulatory regime for an evolving industry. *Washington and Lee Law Review, 69.*

Cohen, J. (2016). *A study on the history and functionality of real estate crowdfunding.* Joseph Wharton Research Scholars, University of Pennsylvania. https://repos-itory.upenn.edu/cgi/viewcontent.cgi? referer = https://www. google.pt/&httpsredir=1&arti-cle=1006&context=josephwhartonscholars.

De Luca, R., & Lucido, N. (2019). *Peer to peer lending: Operational aspects and opportunities for companies and investors.* National Foundation of Accountants.. https://www.fondazionenazionalecommercialisti.it/node/1377

Deloitte. (2016). *Marketplace lenders and banks: an inevitable convergence?* Deloitte Center for Financial Services.

European Bank Authority. (2015, February). *Opinion of the European Banking Authority on lending-based crowdfunding.*

European Commission. (2015). *Crowdfunding explained.* Accessed January 30, 2021, from https://www.europa.eu.

Feth, M., & Gruneberg, H. (2018). *Proptech - The real estate industry in transition.* Available on SSRN: https://papers.ssrn.com/sol3/papers.cfm?abstract_id= 3134378.

Filotto, U. (2016). *Peer-to-peer lending: Myth or reality.* Bancaria Editrice.

Financial Stability Board. (2017). *Financial stability implications from FinTech.* Accessed September 01, 2022, from https://www.fsb.org/.

GAO United States Government Accountability Office. (2011). *Person-to-person lending: New regulatory challenges could emerge as the industry grows.* http://www.gao.gov/new.items/d11613.pdf.

Gilliland, C. (2017, April). *REC What's the buzz?* (Vol. 24). Tierra Grande, Real Estate Center. https://www.recenter.tamu.edu/articles/tierra-grande.

Goins, S. (2014). *Real estate crowdfunding.* Alternative Finance Sector Report at http://www.altfi.com/downloads/real-estate-crowdfunding-report.pdf.

Kirby, E., & Worner, S. (2014). *Crowd-funding: An infant industry growing fast.* Iosco Staff Working Paper No. 3. http://www.iosco.org.

Lehner, O. M., & Harrer, T. (2019). Crowdfunding revisited: A neo-institutional field-perspective. *Venture Capital, 21*(1), 75–96. https://doi.org/10.108 0/13691066.2019.1560884

Lerro, A. M. (2013). Equity crowdfunding. *Investire e Finanziare l'Impresa Tramite Internet.* Il Sole 24 ore Libri.

Marchand, F. (2015). *Equity-based crowdfunding real estate markets.* Working Paper, Delft University of Technology at https://repository.tudelft.nl/.

Matejka, F. (2016). *Venture debt financing for start-up companies.* Master Thesis, Law School Tilburg University. http://arno.uvt.nl/show.cgi?fid=142483.

Milne, A., & Parboteeah, P. (2016). *The business models and economics of peer-to-peer lending.* ECRI Research Report, No 17. Available on SSRN: https://ssrn.com/abstract=2763682.

Moris, J., & Pervaiz, A. (2008, June). *Analysis of the dot-com bubble crisis of the 1990s.* https://papers.ssrn.com/sol3/papers.cfm?abstract_id=1152412.

Morse, A. (2015). *Peer-to-peer crowdfunding: Information and the potential for disruption in consumer lending.* NBER Working Paper n. 20899.

Nash, R. M., & Beardsley, E. (2015). *The future of finance: The rise of the new shadow bank.* Goldman Sachs Equity Research.

Omarini, A. E. (2018). Peer-to-peer lending: Business model analysis and the platform dilemma. *International Journal of Finance, Economics and Trade, 2*(3), 31–41.

Ordanini, A., Miceli, L., Pizzetti, M., & Parasuraman, A. (2011). Crowd-funding: Transforming customers into investors through innovative service platforms. *Journal of Service Management, 22*(4), 443–470.

Pais, I., Peretti, P., & Spinelli, C. (2018). *Crowdfunding: The collaborative path to entrepreneurship.* EGEA spa.

Perkins, W. D. (2018). *Marketplace lending: Fintech in consumer and small-business lending.* Congressional Research Service.

Qian, M., & Hu, F. (2019). An empirical study on prediction of the default risk on P2P lending platform. *IOP Conference Series: Materials Science and Engineering, 490,* 6.

Qi, M., & Yang, X. (2009). Loss given default of high loan-to-value residential mortgages. *Journal of Banking and Finance, 33*(5), 788–799.

Querci, F. (2014). Financial crowdfunding, a new tool for Smes. *Banking, 10,* 26–40.

Schwartz, M. (2016). *Real Estate Crowdfunding 101* (1st eBook ed.).

Schweitzer, M. E., & Barkley, B. (2017). Is *"Fintech", good for small business borrowers? Impacts on firm growth and customer satisfaction.* www.clevelandfed.org.

Sciarrone Alibrandi, A., Borello, G., Ferretti, R., Lenoci, F., Macchiavello, E., Mattassoglio, F., & Panisi, F. (2019). *Marketplace lending. Towards new forms of financial intermediation?* Consob.

Thomas, J. (2014). Making equity crowdfunding work for the unaccredited crowd. *Harvard Business Law Review Online, 62,* https://www.hblr.org//?p=3773.

Tomboc, G. F. (2013). The lemons problem in crowdfunding. *Information Technology & Privacy Law, 30*(2), 253–280. https://reposi-tory.jmls.edu/jitpl/vol30/iss2/2/

Tomczak, A., & Brem, A. (2013). A conceptualized investment model of crowdfunding. *Venture Capital, 15*(4), 335–359.

Vallée, B., & Zeng, Y. (2019). Marketplace lending: A new banking paradigm?. *The Review of Financial Studies, 32*(5), 1939–1982.

Vulkan, N., Åstebro, T., & Sierra, M. F. (2016). Equity crowdfunding: A new phenomena. *Journal of Business Venturing Insights, 5,* 37–349.

Zhao, H., Ge, Y., Liu, Q., Wang, G., Chen, E., & Zhang, H. (2017). P2P lending survey: Platforms, recent advances and prospects. *ACM Transactions on Intelligent Systems and Technology, 72.* https://doi.org/10.1145/3078848

Zvilichovsky, D., Inbar, Y., & Barzilay, O. (2015). *Playing both sides of the market: Success and reciprocity on crowdfunding platforms.* Available on SSRN 2304101.

CHAPTER 6

An Analysis of the Performance of the Proptech Companies

Abstract Proptech companies are not comparable to traditional real estate companies due to the smaller size, the lower initial capital investment, the different business models, and the different economic and financial equilibrium.

This chapter analyzes a complete set of companies active in the proptech industry and compare indexes computed for firms specialized in negotiation, real estate management, and financing services.

Keywords Protech • Balance sheet analysis • Negotiation • Real estate management • Financing

6.1   Introduction

Internet development has offered opportunities to companies that are different from traditional players due to the lower fixed costs and the higher chances to interact in real-time with their customers through apps and websites (Boot et al., forthcoming). Proptech companies are a clear example of technology's opportunities to transform a sector and all the industry players.

Balance sheet analysis in the real estate market is still limited, with few studies pointing out the industry players and the main problems in interpreting balance sheet information (Barkham & Purdy, 1993). A vast

© The Author(s), under exclusive license to Springer Nature
Switzerland AG 2022
G. Mattarocci, X. Scimone, *The New Era of Real Estate*,
https://doi.org/10.1007/978-3-031-16731-7_6

majority of the studies available are focused on listed companies. The research aims to study how the market prices real estate companies and how much the balance sheet information matters (Ooi & Liow, 2002). Proptech companies are mainly unlisted, and no studies allow identifying the main balance sheet features of this type of new player in the real estate industry.

This chapter aims to describe the most critical balance sheet features of proptech companies and point out the main difference among players specialized in negotiation, management, or financing. After introducing the characteristics of the sample (Sect. 6.2), we present the balance sheet indexes selected for evaluating the companies and the main topic of interest for the balance sheet analysis (Sect. 6.3). The balance sheet data is studied by considering the different areas of proptech (Sect. 6.4) separately and comparing the main differences among companies specialized in negotiation, management, or financial services.

6.2   SAMPLE

The sample considers the Proptech companies based in one of the EU 27 countries listed in the Unissu database for which balance sheet data are available on the ORBIS database. The final selection considers 483 based in 22 European countries, as shown in Fig. 6.1.

Countries mainly represented are France (112), Germany (58), and Netherland (57), and there are seven countries with less than five proptech companies with available balance sheets. Companies are analyzed for a ten-year time horizon using their balance sheet data from 2012 to 2021.

The sample is reclassified based on the type of service provided by the corporation by distinguishing Proptech that are offering:

- negotiation activities;
- management services;
- financing solutions.

Companies show some interesting differences in size and the human and capital investment necessary to run the company (Table 6.1).

Companies operating mainly in the management activities are the larger proptech companies for the total assets owned and the number of employees involved. The analysis of the trend in the ten years' time horizon shows that the amount of investment has increased while the number of

Fig. 6.1 Proptech companies' geographical distribution. Source: Authors' elaboration

employees is decreasing, indicating that the equipment/infrastructure expenses have grown over time due to technological innovation. Still, the number of employees necessary for using them is significantly decreased.

Negotiation services do not request a similar size of financial and human resources investment. Still, the role of employees is relatively more significant than the role of assets necessary for offering the service. The substantial improvement in the technology available in the last decade has implied a slight reduction in the number of employees. However, the average size of full-time employees is still from 40 to 50 people.

Proptech financing represents the less human and capital-intensive area, and frequently, companies run with one or two full-time employees. The

Table 6.1 Sample characteristics

	Average total assets (000€)			N° employees		
	Negotiation	Management	Financing	Negotiation	Management	Financing
2012	11,597.23	12,075.91	73.44	61.75	415.23	2.00
2013	9744.88	19,541.12	1576.57	49.83	376.13	2.00
2014	10,891.86	14,918.40	1553.59	67.40	364.49	2.00
2015	10,131.55	11,454.58	1587.90	62.00	268.58	2.50
2016	8320.10	19,125.47	1534.40	51.13	255.95	2.00
2017	16,160.88	29,373.21	1055.55	47.70	273.24	2.50
2018	17,116.26	26,723.55	1028.15	46.69	257.16	2.50
2019	17,951.12	30,635.83	596.52	37.77	266.28	5.33
2020	17,962.08	35,156.85	645.43	30.21	259.25	7.00
2021	23,392.61	51,739.74	261.64	44.50	254.59	1.50
Average	14,326.86	25,074.46	991.32	49.90	299.09	2.93

Source: Author's elaboration

low number attain only the workers directly hired by the proptech company and does not consider all the people that may provide some of the externalized services (IT support, banking services, etc.)

6.3   Methodology

Operational efficiency is studied by considering the composition of short-term assets and liabilities based on the following proxies:

$$Current\ Ratio_{it} = \frac{Short\ term\ assets_{it}}{Short\ term\ liabilities_{it}} \tag{6.1}$$

$$Stock\ turnover_{it} = \frac{Warehouse_{it}}{\dfrac{Operating\ Revenues_{it}}{365}} \tag{6.2}$$

$$Collection\ period_{it} = \frac{Credits\ to\ Customers_{it}}{\dfrac{Operating\ Revenues_{it}}{365}} \tag{6.3}$$

$$Credits\ period_{it} = \frac{Debt\ to\ suppliers_{it}}{\dfrac{Cost\ of\ Goods\ Sold_{it}}{365}} \tag{6.4}$$

The current ratio (6.1) measures the gap of the investment in short-term asset concerning short-term liabilities and companies with higher value of the ratio are less exposed to a risk of lack of liquidity (Bragg, 2003).

The stock turnover (6.2) measures the number of days the current warehouse can ensure to continue production without new procurement activities, and higher values of the ratio identify companies that are investing more in the warehouse (Abascal, 2012).

The collecting period (6.3) measures customers' average time to pay for services or goods already provided. Higher index values identify companies supporting their sales using trade credit as a marketing tool (Jones, 2018).

The credit period (6.4) measures the average delay obtained from the suppliers, and a higher number of average days identifies companies with a more substantial market reputation and bargaining power (Gibilaro, 2018).

The financial structure is analyzed by using the following indexes:

$$Interest\ Coverage_{it} = \frac{EBIT_{it}}{Interest_{it}} \tag{6.5}$$

$$Gearing_{it} = \frac{Short-term\ loans_{it} + Not\ current\ Liabilities_{it}}{Equity_{it}} \tag{6.6}$$

$$Solvency\ ratio_{it} = \frac{Equity_{it}}{Total\ Assets_{it}} \tag{6.7}$$

The interest coverage (6.5) allows understanding the sustainability of the company's debt cost by comparing the EBIT with the annual cost of debt. Healthy firms are characterized by values higher than one in the medium-long term (Damodaran, 2011).

The gearing ratio (6.6) compares the financial debt (short term and medium-long term) with the equity exposure. Higher values of the index identify riskier companies that are more dependent on debt financing concerning equity financing solutions (Massari, 1990).

The solvency ratio (6.7) measures the number of resources invested by shareholders in the company. Higher values of the ratio identify companies where shareholders trust more about the results and are willing to invest a large amount of the necessary overall resources (Hitchner, 2011).

The performance analysis could consider the point of view of all the stakeholders of the company or only the shareholders in formulas:

$$OR\ per\ employee_{it} = \frac{Revenues_{it}}{N°employees_{it}} \tag{6.8}$$

$$Profit\ Margin_{it} = \frac{EBIT_{it}}{Revenues_{it}} \tag{6.9}$$

$$ROA_{it} = \frac{P\ /\ L\ before\ Tax\ \&\ Extr.Items_{it}}{Total\ assets_{it}} \tag{6.10}$$

$$ROCE_{it} = \frac{P\ /\ L\ before\ Tax}{Equity_{it} + Not\ Current\ Liabilities_{it}} \tag{6.11}$$

$$ROE_{it} = \frac{P\ /\ L\ before\ Tax\ \&\ Extr.Items_{it}}{Equity_{it}} \tag{6.12}$$

Revenue per employee (6.8) is a standardized proxy used for evaluating the income produced by the company based on the number of employees involved. Higher values of the index identify more profitable companies and less human capital-intensive ones (Becker et al., 2001).

The profit margin (6.9) measures the percentage of revenues that the company can transform into EBIT. Higher index values identify companies that can run the business by minimizing operational costs (Walsh, 2012).

Return on Asset (6.10) measures the stakeholders' performance by comparing the net performance before taxes and extraordinary items with the total assets and higher ratio values to identify companies that can better maximize the wealth for the stakeholders (Dallocchio & Salvi, 2011).

The Return on Capital Employed (6.11) focuses on the core business. It measures the firm's performance concerning the long-term financing solutions (equity and not current liabilities), and higher values identify more profitable companies (Brunetti, 1971).

Return on Equity (6.12) considers the company's overall performance concerning the financing resources provided by shareholders, representing a proxy of the maximum result achieved by the equity holders (Mella, 1998).

The analysis will consider separately companies classified based on the type of activity in the proptech sector.

6.4   BALANCE SHEET ANALYSIS

6.4.1   *Proptech and Negotiation*

Some unique features characterize proptech companies commonly providing negotiation services in their operation due to the type of service that does not require enormous investments for their core business (Table 6.2).

Proptech companies providing negotiation services typically finance most of their current assets with no current liabilities, and the current ratio is significantly higher than two in all the years considered.

The warehouse is not strictly necessary for running this type of business, and many proptech companies work with no items in the warehouse. This evidence is coherent with the kind of service that does not request an actual "production process" and could be performed with a just-in-time approach.

In 2012, the trade-credit policy was characterized by longer dilation given to customers concerning the conditions applied by suppliers. However, in the last years, the gap has been almost zero due to the increase in the average number of days of delay offered by the suppliers.

The specific features of the business profitability and the assets owned by the proptech companies impact the company's leverage policy (Table 6.3).

Table 6.2 Operational efficiency for proptech companies active in the negotiation activities

Year	Current ratio	Warehouse turnover (days)	Collection period (days)	Credit period (days)
2012	8.49	4.11	65.45	16.84
2013	9.65	4.21	71.94	32.73
2014	6.59	4.85	107.94	40.02
2015	6.59	2.47	67.89	44.16
2016	4.09	5.24	48.52	51.50
2017	4.03	4.457	52.23	46.54
2018	4.94	4.41	80.69	59.41
2019	5.10	3.77	69.40	44.67
2020	2.58	4.60	86.73	88.71
2021	3.17	0.05	50.40	50.86

Source: Authors' elaboration

Table 6.3 Leverage policy for proptech companies active in the negotiation activities

Year	Interest coverage	Gearing ratio	Solvency ratio
2012	57.24	46.49%	59.56%
2013	28.12	50.85%	63.42%
2014	42.21	67.25%	59.62%
2015	63.56	46.12%	62.69%
2016	140.42	91.67%	45.91%
2017	3.65	89.16%	28.95%
2018	51.22	98.08%	35.40%
2019	72.11	12.54%	48.16%
2020	-15.66	116.15%	36.49%
2021	6.83	38.21%	47.61%

Source: Authors' elaboration

Excluding 2020 that due to COVID-19 lockdowns and working from home solution hurts trade and rent of real estate assets and fee revenues, in all the years, the cost of debt is sustainable based on the EBIT produced.

The role of debt is significantly lower than that of equity financing in all the years considered, excluding 2020, which was a great year due to the availability of Government-guaranteed loans that many companies have requested to manage the crisis condition.

Equity financing frequently represents more than 50% of the overall asset even if, from 2015, the role of this source of capital has decreased over time.

The performance analysis of companies active in negotiation services shows an overall negative trend since 2016 (Table 6.4).

Revenues for employee significantly decreased during the ten-year time horizon moving from 329,250€ per employee in 2012 to only 76,590€ in 2022. The negative trend seems not to slow down during the years.

Profit margins are (when positive) from 7% to 13%, and in the period analyzed, the average net income is mainly negative. So all the performance measures (ROA, ROCE, and ROE) have been negative for almost all the years. As expected, losses matter the most when the analysis is focused on the shareholders (ROE) but also for the ROA, the number of years with positive performances is minimal.

Table 6.4 Performance analysis for proptech companies active in the negotiation activities

Year	OR/employee (th€)	Profit margin	ROA	ROCE	ROE
2012	329.25	13.37%	11.61%	-114.73%	58.54%
2013	292.19	12.54%	-7.44%	-9.11%	-10.41%
2014	47.66	11.95%	-0.95%	-7.39%	-1.43%
2015	207.28	7.53%	0.06%	-5.32%	5.97%
2016	197.05	-8.01%	-9.91%	-52.21%	-47.81%
2017	228.89	-11.30%	-6.42%	5.55%	-29.77%
2018	214.57	-2.40%	-0.32%	-0.84%	-17.63%
2019	166.96	-21.45%	-9.40%	-47.16%	-84.52%
2020	147.72	-21.61%	-16.24%	-49.26%	-42.75%
2021	76.59	-26.55%	-5.65%	-16.19%	-50.24%

Source: Authors' elaboration

Table 6.5 Operational efficiency for proptech companies active in the real estate management

Year	Current ratio	Warehouse turnover (days)	Collection period (days)	Credit period (days)
2012	2.66	310.15	92.44	49.26
2013	3.37	119.07	83.88	58.07
2014	3.09	170.85	75.35	47.06
2015	3.16	109.26	75.61	55.81
2016	2.43	230.43	75.44	52.31
2017	3.25	150.51	71.13	43.79
2018	3.33	150.61	70.22	39.70
2019	3.30	220.36	63.88	41.91
2020	3.73	197.09	62.34	40.05
2021	3.36	130.63	49.40	54.10

Source: Authors' elaboration

6.4.2 Proptech and Real Estate Management

Real estate management includes moving from facility management, asset management, and advisory (technical or commercial) activities. However, it is still possible to identify some business features from their balance sheet (Table 6.5).

Real estate management services request a significant investment in the short-term asset, and only half or one-third of them are financed through current liabilities.

Investments in the warehouse are a suitable investment for the companies. The number of assets available at the end of the year allows us to continue servicing the customers for more than three months, even if the value is significantly volatile over time.

Trade credit given to customers is decreasing over time, and up to 2020, proptech companies may be more exposed to liquidity risk because the trade delay obtained by suppliers was lower. In 2021 the average time to pay from a supplier and to customers had been almost the same because the trade policy conditions for suppliers had not changed significantly in the ten-years' time horizon.

The leverage policy of the firms that offer real estate management services may benefit from the characteristics of the assets in a place owned that could represent a guarantee for the financing solution requested (Table 6.6).

The sustainability of the cost of debt is not an issue for the companies that have in the period analyzed a performance (EBIT) higher by more than 17 times the cost of the financial resources.

Debt is not the leading financing solution adopted by the firms, and the role of equity financing solutions is a little bit higher even if the average difference changes year by year. From 37% to 43% of the total assets are

Table 6.6 Leverage policy for proptech companies active in the real estate management

Year	Interest coverage	Gearing ratio	Solvency ratio
2012	68.02	74.27%	39.26%
2013	50.09	69.03%	39.03%
2014	70.71	83.18%	41.94%
2015	34.35	69.66%	41.74%
2016	44.26	71.10%	38.21%
2017	34.57	58.34%	37.93%
2018	30.20	85.24%	37.60%
2019	17.34	78.42%	39.42%
2020	40.11	89.11%	38.68%
2021	36.83	65.76%	43.73%

Source: Authors' elaboration

Table 6.7 Performance analysis for proptech companies active in the real estate management

Year	OR/employee (th €)	Profit margin	ROA	ROCE	ROE
2012	145.92	2.27%	4.04%	11.58%	14.30%
2013	233.53	6.25%	3.10%	6.95%	14.08
2014	157.73	5.90%	1.91%	38.96%	4.63
2015	136.97	2.32%	1.49%	-8.69%	8.60
2016	133.13	0.23%	-0.01%	-8.18%	-1.64
2017	165.90	0.45%	1.84%	-4.82%	7.22
2018	151.55	-0.80%	-0.65%	-8.96%	-22.72%
2019	156.09	-3.65%	-2.05%	-5.40%	-15.24%
2020	153.36	-3.07%	-3.92%	-5.51%	-18.87%
2021	158.75	2.83%	0.34%	-55.69%	-0.74%

Source: Authors' elaboration

financed through equity, and the financing policy is not changing significantly over time.

Real estate management companies have performed better than other proptech companies for both the overall and core business (Table 6.7).

The average revenues per employee vary from 136,970€ to 233,530€, and the profit margin (when positive) ranges from 2.27% to 6.25%. The ROA and the ROE are negative in only four of the ten years considered, while the ROCE is positive only for three years because the contribution of the great activity to the overall performance is mainly negative, and the value of the index is reduced accordingly.

6.4.3   Proptech and Financing

Companies specializing in crowdfunding and peer-to-peer lending are usually the smaller firms among the proptech companies, and their balance sheet presents unique features for their short-term activities (Table 6.8).

The investment in short-term assets usually is higher than the number of resources collected on the same time horizon, even if the value is significantly volatile because the companies do not have a massive investment in the total assets. The companies are run without a warehouse. The customers' collection period is usually longer than the credit period obtained by suppliers. There are some outliers every time the proptech company has to

Table 6.8 Operational efficiency for proptech companies active in the financing service

Year	Current ratio	Warehouse turnover (days)	Collection period (days)	Credit period (days)
2012	2.75	0.00	41.12	36.67
2013	1.10	0.00	15.47	62.65
2014	1.55	0.00	61.00	231.10
2015	1.54	0.00	29.79	75.78
2016	5.00	0.00	99.68	21.81
2017	6.77	0.00	97.88	106.55
2018	6.76	0.00	16.98	62.65
2019	9.44	0.00	36.34	114.71
2020	6.16	0.00	37.15	13.49
2021	2.88	0.00	41.40	31.22

Source: Authors' elaboration

Table 6.9 Leverage policy for proptech companies active in the financing service

Year	Interest coverage	Gearing ratio	Solvency ratio
2012	2.40	189.53%	61.83%
2013	-1.68	132.77%	45.37%
2014	2.35	132.96%	40.06%
2015	-34.35	51.23%	37.40%
2016	-19.50	50.10%	62.07%
2017	-10.11	47.03%	52.24%
2018	-30.79	12.79%	64.94%
2019	-29.55	17.93%	67.83%
2020	-56.59	30.91%	72.18%
2021	-10.19	8.40%	90.20%

Source: Authors' elaboration

buy new IT infrastructure for which the trade-credit conditions are typically less penalizing.

The amount of capital invested for developing a peer-to-peer or a crowdfunding platform is significantly lower than any other proptech company, and leverage policy indexes are affected by this unique feature of the companies (Table 6.9).

The main problem for the companies active in the financing service is the sustainability of the debt cost because firms frequently run at a loss and

Table 6.10   Performance analysis for proptech companies active in the financing service

Year	OR/employee (th €)	Profit margin	ROA	ROCE	ROE
2012	131.29	2.19%	1.59%	10.35%	8.20%
2013	113.54	-4.98%	-18.81%	-24.58%	-46.75%
2014	129.34	1.65%	-5.36%	-7.46%	-3.70%
2015	76.78	8.43%	-0.58%	-11.16%	-3.01%
2016	45.89	-0.40%	-7.28%	-23.82%	-25.75%
2017	15.00	-70.89%	-8.56%	-6.08%	-11.30%
2018	40.18	-6.41%	-28.23%	-29.49%	-60.43%
2019	34.39	-27.82%	-47.90%	-186.70%	-220.83%
2020	96.88	-25.17%	-47.05%	-114.43%	-126.92%
2021	131.78	-18.94%	-7.93%	-13.43%	-10.40%

Source: Authors' elaboration

cannot repay the debt. The role of debt on the overall resources is significantly decreased over time, and on average more than half of total assets are financed through equity solutions.

Proptech companies active in the financing sector are frequently startups, and like all the other companies in this stage of their life cycle, they are run at a loss (Table 6.10).

Revenue per team member is comparable with other proptech companies. Still, the result is biased by the vast difference in the number of full-time workers that in the companies specialized in financing activities is the smallest one.

Companies are run at a loss, and, excluding the anomaly of 2012, all the profitability measures are harmful, and losses are affecting the shareholders among all the company's stakeholders.

6.5   Conclusion

Proptech companies have core business characteristics that make them different from traditional real estate companies, and the impact is on operational efficiency, financing policy, and profitability. The main difference is related to the size of the assets owned and the number of employees that, due to the opportunities offered by the technology, are less relevant to other real estate companies.

Companies that are offering mainly negotiation services are not suffering from liquidity issues, are primarily using equity financing solutions, and can reach a high level of revenue. The main problem for the companies is the cost management that frequently does not allow them to close the fiscal year without a loss.

Proptech companies that are offering services for managing real estate assets are the most common type of firm active in the sector, and in the last ten year, they were also the more profitable ones. The financing policy of these companies is typically using more leverage. They may have more problems related to working capital management due to the longer working capital cycle that characterizes their business model.

Peer-to-peer and crowdfunding players are the small players in the proptech industry. They frequently register losses at the end of the fiscal year and mainly use equity to finance their activity. The company's business model allows them to work without a warehouse and is not exposed significantly to liquidity risk issues.

The empirical evidence provided in the chapter shows that proptech companies are different in their business idea and the economic fundamentals and equilibrium concerning traditional real estate players. Moreover, the balance sheet analysis will provide further evidence based on the company's core business. Identifying a unique standard for the balance sheet structure for all the proptech companies is impossible.

References

Abascal, E. M. (2012). *Finance for managers*. McGraw Hill.

Barkham, R. J., & Purdy, D. E. (1993). Property company financial reporting: Potential weaknesses. *Journal of Property Valuation and Investment, 11*(2), 133–144.

Becker, B. E., Huselid, M. A., & Ulrich, D. (2001). *The HR scorecard. Linking people, strategy, and performance*. Harvard Business School Press.

Boot, A., Hoffmann, P., Laeven, L., & Ratnovski, L. (forthcoming). Fintech: What's old, what's new? *Journal of Financial Stability*.

Bragg, S. M. (2003). *Business ratios and formulas. A comprehensive guide*. Wiley.

Brunetti, G. (1971). Il sistema dei quozienti di bilancio: alcuni caratteri strutturali e funzionali. *Rivista dei Dottori Commercialisti, 4*, 1117–1150.

Dallocchio, M., & Salvi, A. (2011). *Finanza aziendale 1*. Egea.

Damodaran, A. (2011). *Applied corporate finance*. Wiley.

Gibilaro, L. (2018). *Trade credit and financing instruments*. Business Expert Press.

Hitchner, J. R. (2011). *Financial valuation. Applications and models*. Wiley.

Jones, S. A. (2018). *Trade and receivables finance. A practical guide to risk evaluation and structuring.* Palgrave Macmillan.

Massari, M. (1990). Gli strumenti per le analisi finanziarie. In G. Pivato (Ed.), *Trattato di finanza aziendale.* Franco Angeli.

Mella, P. (1998). *Indici di bilancio.* Il Sole 24 Ore Libri.

Ooi, J. T. L., & Liow, K. (2002). Real estate corporations: The quest for value. *Journal of Property Investment & Finance, 20*(1), 23–35.

Walsh, C. (2012). *Key management ratios.* FT Prentice Hall.

CHAPTER 7

Conclusion

Abstract The proptech industry is a fast developing area that is radically changing one of the most important sectors in all the developed countries' real estate. Technology innovation is not expected to slow down in the following years, so the new players will also have a higher probability of being innovative in the future.

The analysis provided in the book has pointed out the profile of proptech firms that mainly operate in the negotiation area, the real estate management, or the financing area. The differences are not only related to their business model but also the economic fundamentals of the corporation.

Keywords Proptech • Negotiation • Real estate management • Financing

The real estate sector is one of the most relevant areas of activity in the world market, and, for some countries, it also represents an investment opportunity for foreigners. The industry, understood as the sum of the investments in construction, spending on rents, and brokerage services, represents a large part of nations' GDP.

The real estate industry is undergoing a digital transformation that changes its nature in terms of the markets and work environments and

© The Author(s), under exclusive license to Springer Nature   135
Switzerland AG 2022
G. Mattarocci, X. Scimone, *The New Era of Real Estate*,
https://doi.org/10.1007/978-3-031-16731-7_7

influences its growth perspectives. Proptech can be seen as a new battleground in real estate. Global technology entrepreneurs and investors have begun turning their attention to reinventing the real estate sector through business models and product innovation.

Proptech is a massive implementation of emerging technology within the real estate sector. So, Proptech is characterized by the massive implementation of emerging technology such as home matching tools, drones, virtual reality, building information modeling (BIM), data analytics tools, artificial intelligence (AI), Internet of Things (IoT) and Blockchain, smart contracts, crowdfunding in the real estate sector, fintech related to real estate, smart cities, regions, intelligent homes, and shared economy.

The proposed analysis has provided the critical concepts of the Proptech phenomenon and evolution over evolved. The proposed research has delivered crucial images of the Proptech phenomenon and its evolution over the years (from 1.0 to 3.0). The study of the new framework has highlighted the opportunities related to Blockchain application in real estate and the role of innovation as a critical driver for the competition in the recent real estate industry.

Proptech's market has been growing fast in the last decade, and, as of January 2021, the total number of companies active in Europe was 633 in which; in the first five countries (France, Germany, the Netherlands, Finland, and Slovakia); there is more than 60% of the total number of Proptech companies active. The development of the market is not homogenous, and some areas (like Contech) are developing fast concerning the rest of the market.

Negotiation activities are among the most requested services for the proptech companies, and the demand is increasing yearly for both the ownership and the renting market. The new order is characterized by a higher role of value-added service (i.e., due diligence) concerning simple advertising on the web.

Real estate management may benefit significantly from using new technology, and users have discovered that the cost-saving opportunities are economically relevant in the short term. Proptech companies are currently very active in this area of real estate, and the number of new companies operating in this area is increasing year by year.

Financing opportunities related to crowdfunding and peer-to-peer represent an alternative financing channel for all companies and sectors. The real estate market is exploiting the advantages of opening the market to web-based investors. Proptech companies are currently working on improving the efficiency of the real estate crowdfunding platforms for both equity and lending solutions. The main issue is adapting their business model to a rapidly changing regulatory environment.

Proptech companies have unique features in their balance sheet because their business is low capital intensive for both financial and human resources. Firms specialized in negotiation activity are less exposed to liquidity problems, but they suffer from a considerable variability in performance over time. Corporations that offer services for managing real estate assets are the more profitable but also more capital intensive. Proptech companies offering financing solutions are low capital intensive but significantly exposed to the risk of losses.

INDEX

GPSR Compliance
The European Union's (EU) General Product Safety Regulation (GPSR) is a set
of rules that requires consumer products to be safe and our obligations to
ensure this.

If you have any concerns about our products, you can contact us on

ProductSafety@springernature.com

In case Publisher is established outside the EU, the EU authorized
representative is:

Springer Nature Customer Service Center GmbH
Europaplatz 3
69115 Heidelberg, Germany